30 REASONS TO SWIPE LEFT

JANE FULTON

Fulton Books Publishing, Scotland, UK.

Every effort has been made to ensure this book is free from errors or omissions. These stories are based on real life experiences from the author and followed by friends' stories at the end.

Disclaimer: All names and locations have been changed, although for some it was tempting to name and shame. Still, I don't want to find myself in a courtroom anytime soon.

These stories are intended to be funny and for the purposes of humour. These experiences are not recommended by the author but if you do attempt any of these yourself please take care and be safe.

Cover Design: Kat Connelly @yer_awrite

Editor: Kirsten Rees | Book Editor & Author Coach

ISBN: 978-1-8384956-0-2

Connect with Jane:

Instagram @swipeforeverafter

Twitter: swipe4everafter

Email: janefultonauthor@gmail.com

To all those who have experienced a dating disaster.

In 2018, I had a thought
I experienced many crazy dates, it was a lot
I began a journal to remind me of those times
Wondering why I didn't leave when I saw all the signs.

Looking back on my life, I questioned my past
Why did I stand by for so long and not get out fast?
Now that I'm older I feel stronger and content
On a mission to find my ideal perfect gent.

Contents

Acknowledgements

Thank you to all the men I have dated. Without all these terrible, odd, wacky dates, I wouldn't have been able to write this book. Eight years ago, I went to a psychic who said I would write a book. In that moment, I told myself that psychics talk a load of shit. I had failed Higher English twice (did worse the second time around), so there was no way I would be writing a book. It wasn't even something I had any interest in … So maybe psychics *are* real. Maybe she could foresee that I was about to begin a dating journey like no other.

To all my friends who gave me feedback when writing my chapters and for also letting me use their dating stories to add to the ending of my book. They made me promise them it would all be anonymous, though I think they got off lightly in comparison to my stories. Thank you to my group of pals, aka Team Blonde (Senga, Louise, and Weejo), who didn't judge me whenever I messaged the group chat about another disastrous date. They always expected any date I went on to not go smoothly, so I provided them juicy gossip, and they were my therapists.

Now onto the boys, it's only right to mention my male friends who were on hand with advice and to give me the male point of view. To be fair, it was always terrible advice, but they were nice enough to let me rant about how the men were arseholes. My friend, Mark, said this book made him realise what a great boyfriend he really is. He also offered a lot of humorous excerpts into my book which were greatly appreciated.

Thank you to my good friend, Gabi, who always gave me positive advice when I was ready to pack in the dating life and head for the nearest convent. Though … she did say the nuns wouldn't accept me as my sins would accumulate to more than the ages of all the nuns put together.

Marissa has been my wing woman and has met most of my conquests. She continually tells me to 'ditch and move on'. Harsh love but solid advice. We all need a Marissa who will tell it how it is - no sugar coating, that's for sure.

My editor, Kirsten Rees, has been a dream and has had her work cut out for sure. I promise I'll try to get a decent qualification in English one day hahaha. She has also been an incredible coach, which has made writing my book not as scary as I thought. My illustrator, Kat, is so talented and has made my book come to life with her illustrations. She's one to watch!

Lastly, thank you for internet dating. Without the joy of swiping and matching, I would not have met most of the men in this book. One other thing I can say for it is that I have also met some incredible men who are now dear friends.

Mr Right, Mr Right, where in the world is my Mr Right?

Glossary

** Higher English: Scottish equivalent to A levels.*

Introduction

Another year has gone by where I'm single AGAIN for all the major events such as weddings, birthdays, Christmas, Hogmanay bells and yes, the dreaded Valentine's Day. The lack of bedroom action is enough for me to get the words 'closed down' tattooed on my vagina. Swipe, swipe, and swipe some more.

With a busy work life as a business owner and not much downtime to socialise due to working well into the evening, opportunities to find love are hard to come by and often occur online. If you take away the perverts, oddballs, fake profiles, and stalkers, it's actually pretty good…sometimes.

Gone are the days when the older generation would meet their future partner on a night out on the tiles, be a gentleman about courting, and within months you are engaged.

It seems technology has taken over and now matching online is the norm. The sound of the ping on your phone, you glance down and see the words appear 'It's a match', woohoo! However, is it really?

Is this new potential candidate who they say they are? Do they even own the puppy they are holding in the picture or is that only for show? Do they really cook or is that a takeaway they've presented on a plate and pretended they enjoyed every minute of whipping up the cuisine. Top chef, my arse! All can seem too good to be true until you meet face to face and find out all you need to know about that person.

I have met what you would class as 'nice guys' until they turn out to have questionable views and tastes. Don't get me started on their bedroom antics. I certainly went in naive and came out wondering why I even explored. Some things are best left undiscovered.

Nearly fifty million people have tried online dating. It is the current trend for finding your ideal partner, soulmate, true love, whatever you want to call them. They say people can spend up to three hours a night on dating apps in search of the perfect match.

I am one of those people who has wasted entire evenings trying to find my future husband when I'm feeling lonely or I've had a long period of abstinence from sex. At times, I have been swiping so fast I'm not even paying attention – it can become robotic. When asked what my type is, the younger me would have been incredibly fussy and have specific requirements, such as 6ft. or above, nice teeth, funny, athletic, good head of hair. Now my type is someone with a pulse who is keen for a relationship. The older you get the more barriers are in the way.

The men I seem to attract tend to be in the following situations.

- Already have kids and against having more.
- Have only ever been in casual relationships as they fear commitment.
- Have already been married and don't want to go through that again.

Now age thirty-five, my chances are looking slimmer. I have been invited to a few weddings next year – there is always hope when I get sat at the singles tables.

If you are reading this book, chances are you are someone who wants to meet your other half, whether it's for fun, casual dating, or a relationship. Or maybe you already have and just want to laugh about how messy dating can get! You know those lonely nights that just seem to creep in? That's when the app gets downloaded or, should I say, downloaded again. There's a thrill to it! It's a rarity to meet someone in a bar, the gym, a club, or through friends these days. It's simply more convenient to download an app and start swiping.

Dating doesn't have to be scary. Yes, it can be exhausting, but it's also fun, interesting, and surprising – you never know what you will get out of it.

This book will give you an insight into the weird, wonderful, and not-so-good side of online dating from a Scottish Lassie*.

There are hundreds of dating apps. The most popular ones include Tinder, Bumble, Hinge, Happn, Match, Badoo, and eHarmony. In fact, eHarmony claims 450,000 couples have found love through their site, and I can believe that! Two of my friends married their Tinder matches and now have Tinder babies (maybe don't tell them I called them Tinder babies).

Some of my friends don't mention to their relatives that they met their partner online. The older generation still seem to question why you would even consider meeting someone through the internet. You can hear their voices saying, 'only perverts and desperate folk are on there.' 'Aye*, all right, Betty! It was easier back in the fifties, when all you had to do was go out dancing, and the following week you were married, and ten years later you had six weans*.'

I've found that, thankfully, opinions are starting to change. Betty would say now, 'did you meet that boy on the Tinder?'

The apps I like are the ones that involve the swipe. Swipe left if you're not interested and swipe right if you like the look of who you see. Once a match occurs – bingo, a conversation can start.

Here is a quick summary of the popular dating sites trending at the moment:

Tinder: When you match with someone, either you or your potential date can start the conversation.

Bumble: Once matched, the woman has to start the conversation. The message recipient has twenty-four hours to respond, otherwise, they are unmatched.

Hinge: Allows you to create an in-depth profile by asking you a series of questions. This allows you to look at other site members' answers to the questions and come up with an opening line.

Happn: You swipe people you have crossed paths with, so if you are attracted to someone you walk past most days on your way to work, you could find them on this app (if they are using it too).

Match: Paid subscription. This caters for people who potentially want to invest in a relationship which whittles out the time-wasters. They also organise singles' events.

eHarmony: Caters for people who are ready to settle down.

Badoo: Uses facial recognition technology to find your ideal partner. Upload a pic of your celebrity crush, and it will aim to find you a similar match.

For those of you who are not overly-familiar with online dating, some apps offer filters so you can select if you want to match with someone who is a particular height, has no kids, is an animal lover, etc.

The initial attraction is based on how someone looks, and once you have both matched with each other, you can dissect their profile and decide if you want to have a conversation.

On your dating profile, there is an opportunity to write a bio, which gives a glimpse into the personality of potential matches. Sometimes, a bio is left blank, which makes things difficult, as you have to think of something interesting or witty to say to the person you find attractive with no clues about their interests. 'Hey, how are you?' after the ten-millionth time doesn't really cut it.

My profile involves a selection of images of me participating in outdoor activities. Once, I uploaded a skydiving pic, and a guy messaged to say when you zoom in you can see my face stretched from the wind – that wasn't the response I was expecting. I was going for the fearless action-girl vibe.

On to the section asking what I am looking for, should I be honest? 'Looking for someone who's an animal in bed, a potential husband who is charismatic, handsome, and confident.' Hmm…sounds too needy, so I opt for: someone who enjoys the outdoors.

The swiping can get exhausting. One time, I actually got finger cramp from continuously swiping left. I used to count how many pictures I viewed before seeing an image I liked of a guy, and it worked out to be roughly one-hundred-and-ten swipes to find one decent picture.

At least with an app, I can open it when I am at home in my pyjamas, or when commuting to work by train, or even while waiting for friends to arrive at a restaurant. Using an app is convenient for me since I have a busy work life.

Here are some of the advantages and disadvantages of online dating:

Advantages:

- Convenient – especially for those who work long days
- Can be picky if you want to be
- Can use app filters to find a better match
- You could meet people outside your social circle
- Access to more potential partners
- Ideal for people who are shy or find it difficult to approach someone

Disadvantages:

- Potentially could end up speaking to time-wasters who are online purely for the ego boost
- Communication online is very different from face-to-face – someone who seems confident online may be really shy in person (or vice versa), which can be off-putting
- People can exaggerate what they do and what they like
- Can be overwhelming as online dating becomes increasingly popular
- Might feel like a competition at times…and not the good kind

The truth is we have now become easily disposable to some. At the first sign of hard work in our dating lives, it is too easy to download the app again and start from scratch. By that point, a whole new catalogue of potential matches is there waiting.

I have suffered a lot in the dating game. Once, I sat through two hours at a Slipknot concert. I was slightly terrified, as the majority of the audience had their faces painted to look like demons and I saw a few people with gimp masks (those saucy minxes).

My date hadn't mentioned to expect this, so it was a shock to my system.

Years later, I was working at a Kiss concert wearing the full face makeup the musicians rock on stage, which I was happy to embrace. It made me realise the slipknot fans must have been buzzing when they dressed up, as that's exactly how I was feeling.

At the rehearsal, Gene Simmons flashed me his nipple which I'm delighted to say, I managed to film on my phone - my Kiss claim to fame. As I sat down at the Slipknot concert, I had a full view of the mosh pit. People were willingly throwing themselves into the pit and I must admit I got a thrill waiting to see if each person would make it out unscathed.

Some serious money could be made betting on who would survive the night blood free. I saw a guy get booted in the nuts and the crowd synchronised by shouting 'Ooooohhh'. I have since found out that there is mosh pit etiquette! If a mosher* sees a punter* about to fall, they will do their darn right hardest to catch that person to avoid injury. Well, from what I witnessed, no one in Glasgow that night gave a fuck as I saw over a dozen being stretchered off by the first aiders. At least it was some distraction, as I genuinely had sore ears from the screaming of the singers on the stage.

Also I pretended one afternoon I was happy to watch an entire cricket match. I've never been so bored in my life. Even got involved in a few fetishes - you'll read more about this later. That said, I have met a few people online who I now call friends. It was a case of realising we enjoy each other's company, but the sexual chemistry wasn't there.

Writing this book has made me realise how much of a people-pleaser I have been. I always want to appear adaptable and don't fuss over anything. The more dates I have experienced, the more

I have come to realise what I want. So, I don't waste my time anymore. If I know it's not going to lead anywhere, then I'm honest. Honesty really is the best policy.

Throughout each chapter, you will read conversations shared with my closest pals aka 'Team Blonde'. The girls have always been on hand to revel in my antics, slag me off and of course lend a supportive ear when required. When we first became acquainted we all had blonde hair, however, our barnet colours began to change just as rapidly as the men in my life! The name 'Team Blonde' stuck despite only one original blonde remaining.

My friends who are in relationships will try to match me up with their single male friends – in some cases for their own benefit, because they like the idea of 'double dates'. Once I was close to agreeing to go on a date with my friend's pal, Peter…that was until we all went to a party together, and I passed out on a bed only to be awoken by him wanking on the bed next to me. Although I didn't tell my friend at the time, I'm sure I'll get a mortified or hilarious phone call from him when he reads this book.

On the subject of wanking, a guy I used to date announced on social media that his father passed away, so out of courtesy, I messaged him to send my condolences. I received an instant response asking if I would come round to his place and stick my finger up his arse. Now, I know people grieve in many different ways but this one had me baffled. He must have got me confused with some other girl who used to go to town on his butt. It would never have been me. I just don't find it a turn-on, and there's that whole fear of getting poo on my finger. Imagine my acrylic nail came off and got stuck up there? No doubt, he's a guy who loves getting his prostate checked by the doctor.

It's also fascinating to me how many people I know in relationships who are too worried about going back to online dating again to risk being single. They would rather continue in an unhappy relationship which they know, deep down, is not right.

The time it is taking me to meet a decent bloke is turning out to be way longer than I had anticipated. I'm a big believer in manifestation and looking for signs. Ask and you shall receive.

I bought a car three years ago, and the salesperson asked if I wanted a three or five-door car. I said three as I didn't have kids and never really had passengers. He convinced me to go for a five-door in case I had kids within the next three years. At the time, it seemed a plausible possibility, so I went for the five-door and not once has a car seat been fitted. In fact, the only regular passenger I have is my dog.

While I might not ever find 'Mr Right', I will search my damned hardest. I want to be with someone I can hold hands with, cuddle up to at night and go on weekends away with. I love seeing my friends gush about their partners, looking at pictures of their holidays, and listening to them share the exciting news that they have got engaged, married, or are having a baby. Okay, well maybe not always hugely delighted. I look at my own life and realise the biggest decision I have to make is which microwavable meal is more appealing for dinner that night.

Everyone has their time, mine might be taking longer to come along than I anticipated, but the thought that I've still to meet Mr Right...well, that's exciting!

Glossary

** Aye: slang for the word yes*

** Weans: term for children/babies*

** Lassie: word for girl*

** Mosher: a person who dances violently or energetically to rock music*

** Punters: another word for people*

Pro/Amateurlogue

Let's start at the very beginning. A very good place to start. My first experience with a relationship was aged eighteen and let's just say I was naive with a capital N. Here I am thinking, you meet a boy, get engaged, married and then have kids. Who even was I back then? How glad I am it didn't pan out like that from the beginning.

The relationship with John started off fun, don't they all! We would find different places to have sex, the riskier the better. We did it at the beach, a park toilet, empty cinema, snooker table, and even on the bonnet of my car.

As the relationship progressed, I started to see how hard work it was to be with him, he was like a toddler. He even took a shit on his mum's doorstep to piss her off. She had locked him out the house one night, as he came back after midnight, and this was his revenge. That wasn't the only time. He destroyed another pair of boxers when he shit himself at a football game. He farted and followed through so disposed of his brown undies in the tank behind the toilet.

I wonder how long they floated there before they were discovered. Yuk!

Our first holiday was a disaster. We headed to Manchester to catch a flight and had hours to spare, so we decided to explore the local area. Unbeknown to me, he hadn't exchanged his money which I reminded him a few times to do (and before you start, I wasn't nagging, it was an encouraging tone). I didn't want to moan at him that he had left this simple task to the last minute, so off we went to the exchange bureau.

It was a miserable day and we had our heavy luggage so we opted to go to the cinema to kill a few hours. Hence why we had sex in the cinema since no one was watching this awful movie which I can't even remember what it was called since it was so shite.

As we left the cinema and headed towards the airport bus, he realised his currency was missing. Turns out he had left his euros in the back pocket of his jeans. He retraced his steps, checked the cinema but they were gone. This was classic John, always quite careless.

John was hyper, always doing stupid things and highly annoying. He was eighteen, so yes, I guess that's how men can behave at that age, but I was more mature and it was hard work being with him at times.

I went to university in England and it was genuinely nice having space, although the idiot in me still travelled six hours every weekend to spend time with him. What was wrong with me? I feel like I missed out on the university lifestyle by sitting on a train, reading books and watching episodes of *Friends* on my portable, seven-inch DVD player.

Before university, he stayed with me at my parents' house which ended up being a relief, as I was sure he would eventually get caught climbing into my window on a daily basis. When I left for my studies, he moved back in with his mum (she eventually forgave him after the shit incident). Although, he did tell me he used to fart on her bedroom pillows if she ever pissed him off, which was a lot.

One evening whilst at uni, my mum called me to say John had let himself into the house at two in the morning with his pal, they had crashed out on my bed. Apparently, he confessed in the morning he had forgotten (in his drunken state) that he no longer lived there. John got away with murder as he had a cheeky grin and he could be hilarious.

He was awful at buying me presents, he got me an ice-cream maker once. We only ever had one ice-cream together so no idea why he thought it would be an exciting present. I like clothes but I don't want a sewing machine to make my own. I like perfume but I don't want to make my own concoction. My friends were getting jewellery, perfume, spa days, etc. and I got this monstrosity. For Valentine's, he got me a scratch card and said that if I won, I had to half it with him.

Hearing my friends boast about lovely gifts they received made me feel disheartened. They had partners who listened to what they liked or admired. I wish he showed a smidge of romance. He was a spender (on himself), he couldn't save but hey no one is perfect.

Three years into our relationship we decided to go backpacking. He was very sociable and could make friends easily. One of his friends flew over to visit us, and on the night he arrived they both got incredibly drunk at a casino and stole money from a machine that accidentally had keys left in it.

They came back to the dorm, next thing I'm waking up to loud banging on the door. *Oh no! What has he done!* John and his pal were escorted out of the dorm by police and security guards. They caught them both on CCTV – they made terrible robbers. As it was the weekend, they were kept in a cell until Monday to see what their outcome would be.

So, there I was, left alone in Australia.

The annoying thing was, on that day we had planned to meet his uncle he had never met, I had to turn up and explain the situation. *Yeah, your long lost nephew has been locked up for stealing money.* It was so awkward. Luckily, I got a free meal which is a positive for a backpacker, money is always tight.

John and his friend were released on Monday with a fine, phew! They both said they really enjoyed their first experience in a cell, as they got to share. They invented a game called sock tennis. Pretty self-explanatory! One of them rolled up their socks into a ball and would throw at the other person who had to whack it back into the hands of the thrower.

"I'm glad you boys were raving it up whilst I was an anxious stressed mess."

Now, there were many other incidents which led to me wanting to leave him. For example, I had arranged for a boat trip to bring the romance back into our lives. John was going out the night before but said it wouldn't be a late evening, specifically reassuring me that he would call me in the morning about catching the boat.

I didn't sleep well as I hadn't heard from him all night and didn't want to message him when he was out with his friends. In the morning, I called him, and it went straight to voicemail. I started to worry. I messaged some of his friends who said he had left early that evening. I was in a total mess. I headed to the harbour in the hope that he had lost his phone and couldn't contact me. I waited an hour.

By that time, I had watched the boat depart. He made up an excuse that he slept through his alarm. Years later, I found out he actually went back to a girl's place. What a slap in the face.

The main turning point was when we decided to move in with a friend, our first experience living together with no adults around. I didn't actually want to move in with him. I wanted to break up with him but didn't want to lose my best friend. That is what our relationship had become. We loved each other's company but for me, the sexual chemistry had gone.

The week before move-in day, we went to see *The Inbetweeners* movie. It was hilarious! He didn't laugh once; that's when I knew something was bothering him and it was the move. If he couldn't laugh at Jay in the movie constantly saying 'clunge' and 'fanny' every two minutes, then something must have been bothering him.

We had a chat in person and decided that it would be best if we broke up. It was upsetting as he had been part of my life for six years. I felt relieved though, no more worrying, stresses, and excuses for sex. It was time to see what else was out there. My poor young self was about to learn many life lessons.

I started going out more regularly to bars and clubs with the girls and got chatted up in the old nightclub Karbon by a guy called Taylor. We flirted, exchanged numbers, I messaged him but never heard back. *Why wouldn't he text back?*

Now bear in mind, I was naïve. I hadn't entered the true world of dating and I certainly hadn't come across a fuck boy*. I had a lot to learn.

Obviously, the next weekend I dragged my friends to the same club in the hope that I'd bump into the same guy, and lo and behold, he was there. Now, fuck boys are confident, can lie well, and are charmers. Before I knew it, all was forgiven: he had been 'very busy at work' (likely, code for busy shagging other girls). That's the stupid kind of excuse I accepted back then.

As the night went on, he invited me and my friend back to a party at his place. Now this was big for me. I hadn't been back to a party with guys I didn't know before. I was slightly scared but my friend said if we didn't like the party, we would leave straight away.

The night turned out to be great, we stayed up drinking and listening to music. My friend and I decided to order taxis at 6am and I persuaded her to get in the first one in the hope that Taylor would kiss me. It worked! We kissed, he said he wanted to see me again, and I left with a crush.

It turned out he must have been 'busy at work' again, as I didn't hear from him. Another three weeks went by before we went back to the club. He was there, and the excuse this time was that he had lost his phone and his contact list didn't save. I knew he was lying but I didn't care as I fancied him. We've all been there when we ignore certain parts of a story to get what we want.

We took a taxi back to his and the night of passion began. Now I hadn't slept with anyone else, I assumed sex would probably be the same (lol). We started going for it and then this odd noise came out of him. A noise that you wouldn't expect from an alpha male. It was high pitched (not quite soprano tones but more alto tones) and he was repeatedly saying, 'heeeee heeeeee heeeee'. He sounded like a sad balloon deflating, or someone on helium who's had bad news. How did I go from having a severe crush on him to wanting him off me?

All I kept thinking about was adding in a harmony to match his tone. I was getting distracted. Should I shout out the word 'man' after he says heeee? Would it work, let's try… heeee man or add a donkey sound so it would be like heeee haw.

Turned out fuck boy wasn't the Master of my Universe.

Now that you've read the warm up, get your popcorn ready, it's time for the show to begin!

Glossary

** Fuck boy: A description of a man who is self-absorbed, doesn't care about a women's feelings and above all, won't commit.*

A single G-string

Have you ever been stuck in a place you can't excuse yourself from? I have. I was dating an American called AJ, which at the time felt exotic and exciting. He was the first person I had dated who was from another country. His Californian tones were a dream, and I could genuinely listen to him talk all day.

What I have realised is that over the years I have adapted my personality to each relationship, almost like a chameleon. I should have owned the music, hobbies, and films I liked. Instead, I pretended I shared his tastes in the hope that he would like me more. It can sometimes take a while to figure out this is the wrong way to try to win someone over.

AJ was into what I can only describe as hippy music. He by no means looked like one – he had the Californian tan, perfect white teeth, and you would hear him before you saw him. AJ was very spiritual and philosophical – I actually enjoyed listening to his theories on the planet and outer space. We would lie in bed watching documentaries. Dating him turned into an education. I would always leave his place more clued up about the world.

He called me up one day, sounding overexcited. One of his favourite singers was in the area, and he had managed to secure two tickets for the gig that night. Apparently, these tickets were like gold dust. He explained the dress code would be very casual, and the venue was intimate so not many people would be attending. He was ecstatic about it and said he was incredibly lucky to have got tickets.

I had been working all day so rushed to meet him after work. If I hadn't been working, I would have checked out the singer's music... Oh, how I wish I had!

Following the postcode on the satnav, it took us to a residential area, no venue in sight. It turned out the gig was being held in a flat. Well, this was going to be interesting. AJ got even more excited. He kept saying it was so typical of this singer, that he was a God and super dope. I began to get excited too – this was going to be a unique event.

We were welcomed into the flat by the 'organiser' who gave us a beer and told us to make our way into the living room. It turned out to be a student flat. The so-called gig was in a bloody* student flat. Now, not to say that every flat owned by students is the same but I could see bongs, lots of empty beer bottles, books under wonky furniture to level out, empty food packets lying around, and an odd smell.

The room's aroma was a mixture of weed and unwashed humans. I wanted to take out my perfume bottle and give the room a well overdue spray.

As we were the last to arrive, the only space left was in the far corner of the room. We had to climb over people to reach it. As I was stepping over people, I noticed people wearing flares, which was ironic as my nostrils were flaring more than any trouser style ever could. Looking around the room, I could see the majority of people had dreadlocks which was a common theme, along with T-shirts emblazoned with slogans like 'vegan is for life, not a trend', 'save the bees', 'peace'. I was wearing a black leather skirt with boot heels; I guessed they were all appalled at my clothing choice, going by their stares towards me. I stood out like a sore thumb.

The musician finally made his entrance into this tiny room, and the crowd of twenty people looked at him as if he was their king. I felt like I had stumbled into a cult. He sat down, closed his eyes for what felt like an eternity then played a string on his instrument. He played one bloody string…and everyone went bonkers*.

It was cringe and uncomfortable, a bit like my very own G string, which was now riding right up my arse due to how I was sitting because of how cramped the room was. Girls, you will totally get how difficult it is to subtly and gracefully dig out your thong from your derriere. I looked at AJ, and he was so into the 'music'. What had happened to him? I was experiencing a side of him I had never seen before.

For the two hours – yes, two hours – I will never get back, I had to entertain myself by counting how long each silence was between each string he played (it was about a minute). I counted the number of objects in the room. I saw Lego figurines on the shelf and some oddly titled books, such as *How to Disappear Completely and Never Be Found.* If only I could find a way to grab this book so it could magically transport me out of this dump.

At one point, I even contemplated swaying like the other punters; I mean, it's a good way to exercise the old joints. I was stuck in that room with nowhere to go, and the only way to get through it was to sway and hum with the others. I rocked back and forth and imagined I was doing my abdominal exercises. I thought maybe I'd at least have a six-pack by the time I left - got to think of the positives in every awful situation.

The room would have been so much more bearable if some people had considered a wash. They should have given out goodie bags at the end filled with bars of soap, hairbrushes, perfume, and wet wipes. I would have happily nominated myself to give them out and spread the message that washing produces the entertaining spectacle of seeing the dirt fall off you in the shower.

Now, back to the musician – though, he should be embarrassed to call himself one. I wanted to grab his guitar and strum *two* strings just to see the reaction from the crowd. Could I be their new God? My first commandment would be for everyone to immediately go for a shower then a haircut and, lastly, a dentist appointment.

The evening got a tad more bearable when a girl brought out a tambourine. A tambourine is upbeat! Unfortunately, it was just a tap here and there, but at least it was something new.

I don't take drugs, though for the first time, I was tempted to find some sort of escapism. I was trying to work out where the smell of weed was coming from so I could snatch the bag. I wouldn't have known how to roll a joint, but by this stage, I would happily have swallowed the whole bag if it would knock me out.

When the cult ceremony, sorry 'gig' finished, I have never wanted to run out of a place so fast. AJ wanted to speak to the musician. About what? What could he possibly have to say to this so-called musician? 'Oh, hey dude, your work is inspiring; that one strum really gets me in the moment?'

A student announced that CDs were on sale, you've got to be kidding! If anyone bought a CD as a present for someone they would think it wasn't working from the lack of music on it.

Luckily, AJ's work visa was about to run out, so I used that as an excuse to not see him again. Hasta la vista, baby!

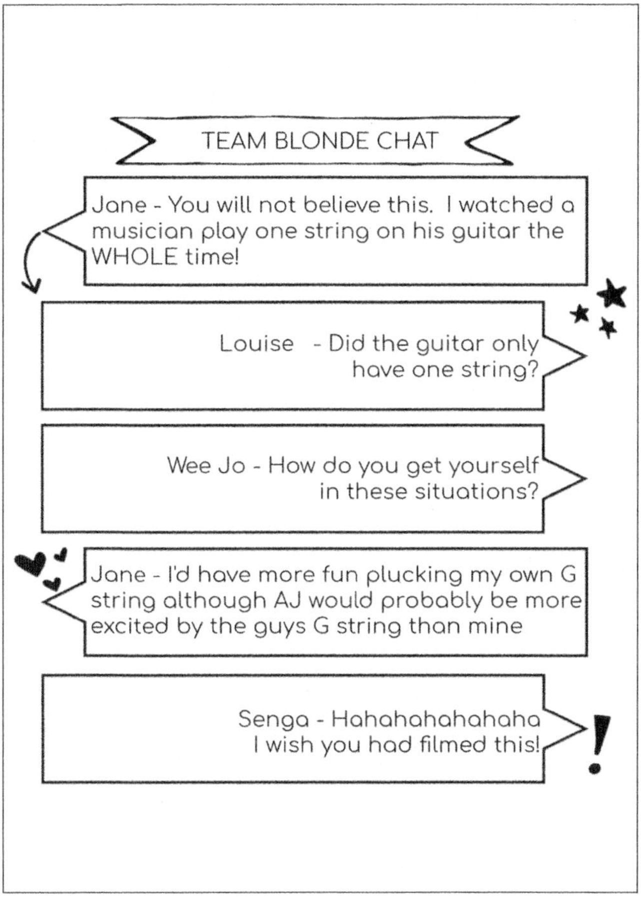

Tips

1. If you're invited to a concert, check out the music beforehand. If you know it's not for you, you can turn down the invitation. How I wish I had done that!
2. If you feel stuck somewhere and desperate to get out, whether it's a concert, comedy gig, theatre show, anything, then GO! You can say you're not feeling well,

or you need the toilet. Once free, RUN for it. Time is precious – don't waste it.

3. Be yourself. Don't try to change your tastes to fit in with your date. AJ didn't like pop music; he went on about how awful it was. The irony when I'd kept my own mouth shut about how much I hated his music all that time. I love pop music yet pretended I wasn't keen so he wouldn't judge me. Always be true to yourself. After all, opposites attract.

Glossary

** Bloody: a word used to intensify what you are talking about*

** Bonkers: mentally unbalanced*

** Shite: describing something that is bad*

Jack in the box

I tend to date men my age or older. I have dated younger men in the past and in my experience, their immaturity always came through. After much persuasion from a friend who was dating a guy five years younger, I decided to temporarily change my age settings on the app to four years below my age.

After a few too many swipes, I came across a guy called Leon who smiled in every pic he uploaded. It was refreshing to see images that were not the standard list: guy with his top off, pouting, selfie in front of a mirror, gym pic. Leon seemed happy and bubbly. Our conversations were going well; he made me laugh and seemed mature for his age – maybe my friend was right about the younger guy thing…

We swapped numbers and arranged to meet the following weekend. A couple of days later, I was driving home from work (it was a sunny day in Bonnie* Scotland – one of the rare days us Scots can catch our vitamin D) when Leon called to ask if I happened to be free to meet him that afternoon instead. I loved the spontaneity of his suggestion, and it was a glorious day. He suggested a walk around his local park then a spot of food at the nearby beer garden. It sounded ideal.

As I approached him in the park, he looked anxious. I thought Leon must be nervous, which I found endearing. How wrong was I!

While we walked through the park, he was constantly texting and not paying much attention to what I was chatting about. His phone kept ringing, but he kept declining the call. I told him to answer next time it rang. He answered the next call and walked away from me so that I couldn't hear the conversation. I began to think something wasn't right. Why ask to meet up with me when he was clearly preoccupied with something else? I was beginning to get annoyed and was not into this date at all.

Leon got off the phone and asked me if it would be okay to meet his sister who was also in the park. Why was his sister in the park? Something weird was going on.

Does he tend to have a relative present at every milestone? Is his sister arriving to vet me on the first date? Will his mum be present the first time he cooks for me? Or worse will his second cousin be watching us and taking notes the first time we have sex?

He and his sister had something they needed to do together quickly. It wouldn't take long. In fact, it was the real reason he had asked me to meet him today. What was he about to say? What could it be that prompted him to get me to come to a park and meet his sister on a first date?

Go on, I thought, *hit me with it…*

He then blurted out that his cat had died, and he was meeting his sister to bury it in the park.

What? He had invited me to a cat's funeral! A pet's funeral on a first date?

My instant reaction was to laugh – this was clearly a wind-up. It was hard not to laugh as I kept thinking 'the cat is definitely out the bag now'.

Leon looked at me in disgust and said he didn't appreciate me laughing at the situation. Er… you have invited me to a cat's funeral, what kind of a reaction were you expecting? He responded by telling me that his cat's name was Jack, and he had been like a brother to him.

Now, I totally get that a pet is a part of the family, but that was not the issue. The point was that this situation was insane. How could he not understand that? His phone rang again. He put it on speaker, and I could hear his sister shouting, 'Where are you? I'm waiting here with Jack in this shoebox like an idiot.'

I was convinced I'd been set up. I stormed off and started looking around, expecting my friends to jump out of the bushes shouting, 'You've been punked' but nope, nothing like that happened. I was just experiencing the most surreal first date.

Leon didn't come after me. Well, I did disrespect his now deceased wee 'bro'. No hard feelings though, since he did have something more urgent to attend to.

Later, I looked him up on Facebook. Sure enough, wee Jack had passed. I sometimes wish I had attended Jack's funeral. It would have been interesting to see how that played out.

Would we throw cat litter on the box instead of dirt?

Would there have been a song? I could play a lovely ballad whilst hitting only one string every ten minutes. Or would Cat Stevens music be playing?

Would other cats have been in attendance?

I will never know. RIP Jack.

TB Chat

Jane – I thought you guys had set me up today – I was invited to the guy's cat's funeral, not making this shit up. I swear I must have been evil in my past life. I was walking out the park looking for you guys to jump out at me with a camera
Weejo – You're lying, this can't be real
Jane – Oh trust me, I'll screenshot his Facebook to show his cat actually died
Senga – Please say you attended this funeral
Louise – I can't cope with this, literally tears running down my face

Tips

1. Avoid meeting the family on a first date – too much, too soon.
2. If your date is constantly looking at their phone then their mind is clearly on something else. Be prepared for the date to not go well.
3. Be sensitive when someone declares their pet has died, no matter what circumstance you may be in. Don't make jokes! I repeat, do not make jokes!

Glossary

** Bonnie: beautiful*

Cumgratulations, that's a record

Now there have been a few men who ticked all the boxes right up until it was time to get intimate. I had been on several dates with Robin, and they had all been perfect. We had an adventure date at Go Ape outdoor centre and a romantic picnic on a hilltop. He even drove me to a picturesque spot to watch the sunset. He was really on the ball with choosing where to go on dates and was very spontaneous. Finally, I felt I was getting closer to finding the ideal man. Robin had no weird habits, he had great conversation, and I felt comfortable enough to want to take it to the next level. As the Americans say, it was time to go for the 'home run'.

Robin invited me to stay over at his. I was feeling excited. After all those fun dates and lots of flirting, I was ready to pounce on him. On arriving at his flat, I could smell the incredible aromas from the meal he had cooked for us. I looked over at the table in the living room and saw he had lit a candle and there was a glass of wine waiting for me. He was melting my heart.

After dinner and a few glasses of wine, we began kissing and ripping each other's clothes off.

If his kissing was that good, I was thinking, bring on the rumpy pumpy. I remembered I had Spanx* on, so I made an excuse to go to the toilet to take them off. I didn't want him to start rummaging around down there and stumble across my big panties.

Now, for all those ladies who have worn Spanx, you will know how difficult they can be to take off. There I was in his bathroom, struggling to get them off. How had they suddenly got tighter? They were literally stuck to my skin. It was like that scene in the series Friends when Ross has his leather pants stuck to him. Similar to him, I was panicking and looking around his bathroom to see if there was some lotion or Vaseline in the hope it would help them slide off.

I resorted to lying down on his bathroom tiles (which were freezing by the way) and tried to wiggle my way out of them – you know, like when a caterpillar sheds its chrysalis to blossom into a butterfly…

By this point, I had built up quite a sweat on my front and frostbite on my back from the tiles so was looking nothing like a beautiful butterfly. When they eventually came off I was not only exhausted, I realised I would now be wearing no underwear. How was I going to explain this to him? I decided I was going to have to walk out of the bathroom naked and pretend I was trying to be sexy for him.

When I walked out, Robin's jaw dropped to the floor – brilliant, it worked! – he reached into his top drawer to get some protection – always appreciated and shows they are respectful. We were ready to go… literally ten seconds later it was over, done, complete. Okay, I get that men can get overexcited, but ten seconds? It wasn't like it was his first time, and he wasn't eighteen. He was a thirty-three-year-old man who had been in relationships.

It was our first time getting intimate, so I reasoned it could only get better, right? When he was ready to go for round two, the same thing happened again.

Oh no! Not again.

He didn't even acknowledge it; he just reached for another condom. By this point, I was no longer turned on. I told him we should try another time. He started kissing me again and – yes, you guessed it – he put on one, two and a third. I started to wonder if I needed a clicker counter to keep track of how many times he produced another.

DING DING DING, rounnnndddd number 28!

The only other time I've been in a situation where a guy has gone through loads of condoms was when the guy was too large in that department and none of my purchases would fit him. As we were going at it and my breasts were swinging about like window wipers, he yelped in pain. He said it was too tight, and it was becoming painful on his knob.

I had a mixture of Johnnies in my top drawer, ranging from scented, lubricated, ribbed, super thin and even a glow-in-the-dark one. He tried different ones on, and each time, the yelping would begin again. He complained that every condom he tried suffocated his shaft, it's the only time in my life that I've seen that shade of purple, his dick was angry at me and no one wants to be faced with one of them.

Before we knew it, my drawer was empty of wrappers and there was a lovely selection all gathered together on the floor. To be honest, I was relieved. I panic when I see a 'large' one (more on that later). I want to be able to walk the next day and not look like someone has been going to town on my internal organs. My drawer now has an assorted pack of all sizes in case that situation should arise again.

On the subject of condoms, the purpose of them is fantastic, yes. But the awkward moment during foreplay when the intimacy is getting heated and then the pause happens when the man goes to fetch a cock sock. That delay can make your moist vagina go dry, like a nun's lady garden of Eden. It can even be humiliating for the man if he struggles to get the cum catcher on.

When you don't know where to look. Should you offer to help? Start playing with yourself? Look away to stop him from being embarrassed? It's always best to have a supply ready and waiting in your top drawer next to the bed.

One time, I had a guy go soft when putting on the condom as it took him ages to find one, then he took his time putting it on. I watched him try to make himself hard until finally, his little one was ready to stand at attention.

Now, back to Robin.

I wanted to give him a useful tip by suggesting he got his condoms from the local sexual health clinic where they were free to save him racking up a huge bill. He was definitely someone who needed access to a large supply of freebies. This was the first time I had cum, I mean, come across someone who suffered from premature ejaculation.

According to netdoctor.co.uk, 'an estimated 30% of men suffer from Premature Ejaculation at some point in their life. Premature ejaculation occurs when a man experiences orgasm and expels semen soon after sexual activity and with minimal penile stimulation. It has also been called early ejaculation and rapid ejaculation'.

After several attempts, I had no desire to try again. I felt bad for him but this wasn't going to work for me. I also didn't want him to waste his rubbers – poor guy would probably end up broke if I let him carry on. It was such a shame. I didn't even know if there was a cure for this condition, though I have since discovered there are treatments.

He then suggested we focus on me – result! However, he asked that I did something for him first. Rude, since he had already been keeping me waiting. Anyway…Robin asked me to start rubbing his nipples. Before that day, I didn't even know men could have sensitive nipples.

I mean, what about mine? Oh well, let's get you going again, Robin. Let's work on your nipples this time, not mine.

I started rubbing his teeny, tiny nipples. He made a groaning noise and shouted for me to do it faster. Now, the face you're making while reading this is probably the same face I was trying hard not to make. I froze. So, he took over and started rubbing his own nipples. He was going for it at full pelt. I genuinely worried his nipples were going to bleed with how hard he was rubbing.

Dude, I thought, *you are going to give yourself a nasty burn if you keep that up.*

His mouth opened, and he orgasmed again, just from rubbing his nipples. Holy shit! The noise he made when orgasming was like a yodel. He held his sound effects for a long time, until I was ready to applaud like they do at the end of a ballad in a concert. He had in total orgasmed five times, while I had received a big fat zero. He started to edge towards me, but I had seen enough. I didn't want him anywhere near me. I had had enough of this surreal experience.

At least I didn't have to do the cum run. The cum run is when a man has shot his jizz inside you and you have to work out how to get to the toilet without it pouring out of you. Classy, I know. You would love to cuddle up after sex but the thought of the sticky liquid pouring down you any second isn't pleasant. So you prep and in your head you gear up for ready, steady, and go!!! You waddle like a penguin to the toilet whilst completely in the buff, cupping your bits, squeezing your pelvic muscles so hard. Proud you can do this but also knowing you won't be able to hold on much longer. You see the toilet and you can relax, ahhhhh.

The downside to this, is that it can sometimes sting when the pee comes out. Once all cleaned up, a surprise can suddenly appear hours later when a rush of liquid fills your pants, those wee penis coladas still swimming about up there have finally given up. Vaginas are complicated in many ways.

A lot goes on down there. First of all, every month we lose about two ounces of blood which often leaves women exhausted, moody and bloated during their period. We also need to open our fannies* not just for sex but for smear tests/STI checks. Essentially, we have to get used to being comfortable with the uncomfortable. Pelvic exercises are a must or pee can slip out when we sneeze or cough. Also once a baby is pushed out of you, the vag might not look the same which is absolutely fine but not everyone feels as confident about themselves after any change.

Friends have told me their beavers look like a lasagne that has been put through a tumble dryer. Us ladies also need to experiment with our noonies* to work out how to orgasm which can be challenging in itself, never mind when a man takes over: A penis must be really easy to deal with, a wee wash in the shower, a wee rub, it's erect, and before you know it you've shot your load. Simple!

There you have it – seemingly perfect partners can turn out to be far from perfect once you get to the intimacy stage. The saying, 'Try before you buy' was finally making sense. Let's go back to the olden days when your first intimate moment with your husband was on your wedding night. Imagine he had what Robin had, visualise how gutted you would be, a lifetime of unfilled sex.

I actually know a girl who waited until her wedding night to have intercourse. During a sleepover, she confessed that before she got married, her boyfriend would put a condom on and rub up and down her but not insert his penis inside her. They certainly had some willpower, at least she got to see his cock before the big day.

That's another thing, imagine on the night of your wedding and your man pulls out a little chipolata, a schlong it was not. On your wedding day, your vows go along the lines of 'To have and to hold, from this day forward, for better, for worse, for bigger, for smaller, in sickness and in health, until death do us part'. Well, you're basically royally screwed if you have vowed those words and have a guy who cannae* use it effectively.

I don't know anyone who's enjoyed their first night of passion. The word passion is far from it. Most of us are aiming to get it over and done with. Purely to say you are no longer a virgin, the cherry has been popped or men will use the Pinocchio quote, "I'm a real boy now".

My first time took a while. I made him wait three months as he had a very big willy (that's what I used to call it back then before I was grown up enough to say the word penis, cock, dick, boaby* etc.). What a way to experience my first time. It was sore, not romantic, I bled and afterwards I thought, *Is this it?* I looked down at the sheets and there was blood, I panicked as I didn't want him to see the blood. Whilst he was in the toilet, I flipped the mattress only to see more blood. *How had my blood soaked all the way through?* Years later when I brought up my sheer panic at the time he laughed and said he had a nose bleed the week before. He had flipped the mattress as he thought that was the best way to deal with it instead of cleaning it.

In the movies, you see the actors panting and making it look like the most desirable thing to do. Well now I know it is, however, your first time though is anything but. I know a guy who felt so much pressure to have sex at age nineteen that he shagged a thirty-two-year-old he met in a bar and pumped* her at a bus stop to get it over and done with.

At least the next person who dates Robin will never be stuck for his ideal gift – a bumper supply of condoms and some Vaseline to keep that nipple rash at bay.

I wanted Batman and got his sidekick.

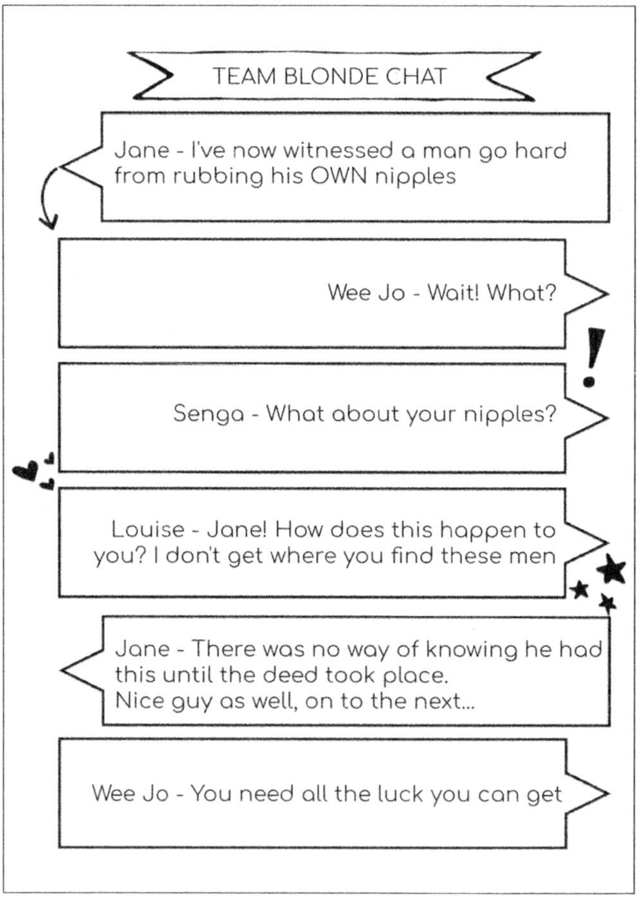

Tips

1. Using thicker condoms can reduce sensitivity and help sex last longer.
2. There are two potential treatments for premature ejaculation – EMLA cream and Priligy tablets. EMLA cream reduces sensitivity by numbing the penis, whereas Priligy tablets help to gain better control of orgasms. But everyone is different so I highly recommend speaking to a doctor about treatments that are available that can help gain better control of orgasms.
3. Some men find that behavioural strategies like the start–stop technique and the squeeze technique help them. I recommend learning to be good at everything else – if you have the foreplay sorted then there's less emphasis on the sexual act itself.

Glossary

* *fannies: also known as a vagina*
* *noonie: another word meaning vagina*
* *cannae: Scottish word for cannot*
* *pumped: another word for shag*
* *boaby: Scottish word for penis*

Caught in a trap

I began to have a suspicious mind indeed. I have had many dating disasters, but surprisingly, this hasn't put me off dating. I mean, there's only so many men I can date before one of them turns out to be my Prince Charming. Disney does have a lot to answer for. Every movie they portray that the prince gets the princess and they live happily ever after. Maybe it's time to explain in schools that not everyone will get their happy ending. Might as well be straight with them, educate them early so they are prepared for the liars, cheats, etc…I know I'm sounding bitter here but I was all bushy-tailed leaving school thinking that true love would be easy.

I had been dating David for a few months, this was a short time after Robin. We had met through a mutual friend. I was hesitant at first, because he was one of those 'clean eating' types, but he liked to binge on the weekends, and that was when we mainly spent time with each other, so it worked out perfectly.

Dating David was going well. So well, in fact, that I felt like we would soon become official. He had told his parents about me, he had introduced me to his friends, he wanted to plan a holiday with me, and he would surprise me with gifts. Finally! I'd met a decent guy. Well, so I thought.

One weekend, I had planned to stay at his, but he cancelled at the last minute. He said his friend Stuart wanted to catch up as they hadn't had a boys' night out in a while. Now, he and this pal worked together so they saw each other all the time. It was annoying that he cancelled our plans with so short notice, but he said he would make it up to me and we'd spend the next day together.

As I was already all dressed up, I asked around my friends to see who was free for a night out. My friend, Marissa, said she'd thought I was going to be at David's. I explained the situation, and she went silent. Silence isn't good. Marissa knew Stuart from when we had all met up for drinks before. She mentioned that she had just seen Stuart on her friend's Instagram story, and they were out together for dinner. I convinced myself that Stuart was on a date but would be meeting David after.

I texted David saying that I was out with the girls and asked if he and Stuart wanted to catch up with us at some point. He replied saying he and Stuart were currently at his place drinking and probably wouldn't be going out now. They were going to order a takeaway. Now I knew he was lying. I was gutted. I didn't know what to do. Maybe the Instagram story was old or from earlier on in the day? My friend checked again. It was recent and another picture had been added. I was devastated; I had had no doubts about the relationship, and I felt like it was going so well. I decided it was time to catch him out.

I called him, but there was no answer. I messaged him saying I knew a girl who was on a date with Stuart – what was going on? After hours, he got back to me and said he was sorry for lying, but he wanted a weekend to himself and hadn't wanted to offend me.

David and I were only seeing each other on weekends due to our schedules, but we spoke every day, so I felt like the trust was there. It didn't make sense. Why couldn't he be honest and just tell me that? I wouldn't have been annoyed at all. He asked me to come round to his place the next day, he wanted to apologise in person and spend the day with me. As much as I was gutted that he didn't want to hang out with me that evening, I was happy that he was at least keen enough to want to make up for it the next day.

The following day, he greeted me with flowers. We went for lunch and to the cinema. It was one of the best dates I had spent with him. I believed I had nothing to worry about; he was obviously telling the truth. This is the moment I wish I could go back in time and shake myself. Currently have my head in my hands at my idiocy.

Instead I went home that night, stress-free and secure in the relationship…until my sister called to say she had matched with David online. My sister had never met him but had seen pictures. She said she saw him, swiped, and they matched. I was mortified. I convinced myself it must be a fake profile, because we had been having such a great time together.

I called him, and I actually laughed when I told him there was a fake profile of him online (lol) and my sister had matched with him. There was that horrible silence, again. Great! Twice that week with the silence of doom. Defeated, he told me he was so sorry but it wasn't a fake profile. He felt the relationship was getting too serious, and it had made him question whether he wanted a girlfriend. He knew that if he asked me to be his girlfriend then I would be the one he would end up marrying, and he wasn't sure if he was ready to settle down. *I smell bullshit.*

It was upsetting to hear this, and it's not the only time this has happened to me. There are other guys I have dated who won't appear in this book, because their only fault was their inability to commit. In my experience, there is always a reason behind this though. People who say they have commitment issues are probably covering up the real reason.

Reasons why people have commitment issues:

- Prefer to be independent and worried if they meet someone, they will have to change their ways
- Too picky
- Hurt from a previous relationship
- Fear of failure
- Inability to share their life
- Want to keep their options open

I guess David wanted to see what else was out there and not put all his eggs in one basket. The grass isn't always greener on the other side, David.

At the time, I was devastated, but if your potential partner is not ready for a relationship then there is nothing you can do. Six months later, he got back in touch to say he had made a mistake and missed me. *Oh hello, ready to beg now are you?* I told him I wasn't sure and we were best to meet up and talk. So many months had passed, I wasn't even sure if I would feel the same.

The following week an announcement appeared on Facebook. His status showed he was in a relationship, *what?* I messaged him to figure out what was going on. Turns out he had been friends with this girl for years, they had been on dates on and off, and decided to make it more serious.

Did he forget he told me he wanted me back?

He is now married to that girl and they have a kid (and he messaged me whilst she was pregnant asking to hook up).

Go figure! Another one bites the dust.

TB Chat

Jane – Well that's the end of me and David, I'm actually gutted
Louise – Oh no! What happened? You really liked him as well
Senga – I'll be round with the pizza and ice cream
Jane – Commitment issues, I mean I wasn't asking for marriage
Weejo – Sorry Jane, that's shit. I'll organise a girls' night
Jane – If I go out, I'll be giving all men the evil eye. Why are some men a bag of dicks!

Tips

1. If you receive flowers after catching someone out in a lie, they are almost certainly ballsguilty, just saying.
2. If your partner is spotted on dating apps, then as much as it hurts, they are over their relationship with you.
3. Never ditch your friends when you have a partner. Your friends will always be there, while partners can come and go. It was thanks to my friend that he was caught out. Besties before testies.

Rub a stub stub

After a break from online dating, I thought it was about time to give it another whirl. I got chatting to Martin who was from a small island off the north coast of Scotland. I was fascinated by his stories about growing up in a place that has a low population and the first language is Gaelic. A date was set, and I was feeling incredibly nervous. The conversation online had been flowing well; I prayed that it would be the same when we met.

I always give myself too much time to get ready before a date. I then end up clock-watching, deciding when it is best to leave my flat. Should I be five minutes late? On time? Early? I overthink too much on a first date.

Martin and I had decided to meet for dinner. I saw him standing outside in the rain, and he looked exactly like his picture. Actually, he looked better – phew! I found it endearing that he was willing to get drenched in the rain while waiting for me.

This is when I play out a romantic scene from a rom-com in my head and convince myself that this date is going to be perfect.

I felt very comfortable around him; he had a lovely smile, great hair and a bushy beard. Now a bearded fella is not my type at all, but I had seen one of his images online that showed him without a beard – he had looked insanely handsome. If we started dating, I could always try to persuade him to get the trimmer out and say bye-bye to his hairy friend.

During dinner, we couldn't stop laughing at all our dating disaster stories. We seemed to be on a par with the number of oddballs we had come across. He was funny, charming and handsome; I was really hoping there would be a second date, until he suddenly announced he had an interesting fact about himself.

Martin put his hands out in front of me and asked if I could see anything unusual. My first instinct was to look for a scar – growing up on an island, you would probably have to find some pretty wild activities to amuse yourself. Maybe, Martin's adventures had left him close to death's door and he had a story to tell? Perhaps, he was about to do a magic trick? I had already started to imagine what other kinds of tricks he might have up his sleeve …

I flipped his hands over and couldn't see anything unusual. He then grabbed my fingers and placed them on his pinkies. There were lumps on either side of his pinky fingers. Oh no! What was he about to reveal?

'I was born with twelve fingers. Go on, feel my lumps,' Martin said.

Feel the lumps? How was this happening to me? Should I go for it and start rubbing the stubs? Should I look at him in disgust? Should I laugh? I didn't want to hurt his feelings. So I thought, *here goes.* There I was, sitting in a nice restaurant, stroking his pinky stubs while I watched his eyes start to roll back in ecstasy.

My question is why? Why does weird shit happen to me? Why do I attract men who instantly open up on a first date and tell me too much personal information? It's not the hairdressers, where we often share way too much! I look around me and desperately hope any girl can see the look of horror on my face and will feel sympathy and offer to swap places with me. Someone make eye contact with me. Please for the love of God, help a sister out.

My order to the waitress is, can I have the man she has as mine isn't quite what I expected. At first glance, it was presented well and interesting to look at, now that I've looked more closely there are extras I didn't order. Now I'm worried if I continue with what I have in front of me, I will see something more unpleasant. I wondered, if I rubbed hard enough, would a genie magically appear and grant me three wishes? Or should that be twelve wishes? Was this how his foreplay started? A girl would start to rub his shaft, and he would move her hands to either side of his stubs instead. There you are ladies, to turn him on just rub his stubs…

He explained that his siblings were also born with twelve fingers. Certain thoughts were starting to pop up in my head. I had to restrain myself from having vocal diarrhoea on him and blurting out 'inbred' and 'your mum's a brother shagger'. There had to be a blood relation somewhere in his parenthood. I had to think rationally.

I gave myself a pep talk and reminded myself that he was a lovely, funny guy and that he didn't have twelve fingers now. *Would it even matter if he did?* It's rare enough to meet a 'nice guy', and with his abnormality, he was even rarer. As they say, diamonds are rare, and they are precious. If you're born with extra fingers or toes, it's called polydactyly. It's genetic.

Maybe I should give him a chance?

I imagined if he still had those extra digits and thought of the positives:

- He might be an incredible pianist or harpist.
- He could make a decent basketball player.
- Being intimate could be interesting.
- He could fit more Hula Hoop crisps on his fingers than anyone else.

Making light of the situation felt like the way to go. After the stroking of his stubs, it was time for the bill, and he offered to pay. I always find paying the bill very awkward, because I don't ever want a guy to think I'm one of those girls who expects to be paid for. When the card machine arrived, he brought out his bank card and a piece of paper from his wallet that had his PIN on it. Martin explained that it was a new card, and he had written down the PIN, as he hadn't memorised it yet. It was just four digits though. I know my National Insurance number, mobile number, bank account number and sort code, even my first home telephone number from twenty-five years ago, and he couldn't remember four digits?

After three declines, I offered to pay to avoid any embarrassment. He couldn't even write down the four-digit number correctly. It totally killed the mood, but I talked my way round by reminding myself that he was probably mortified and decided not to judge him on that one incident – these things can happen. I didn't want to be overly picky, and the first date can always be fraught with nerves. He asked if we could meet again, and I decided to oblige.

The following weekend, I was at a wedding reception, and he was out with friends at a bar nearby. We agreed to meet after 1 a.m. once the reception was over. Midnight came, and I looked at my phone – there were seven missed calls from him. Calm your panties you needy Nancy. I messaged him asking if he was okay, and he said he was outside waiting for me. I explained that I wasn't leaving until 1 a.m. Of course he said he would happily wait – first sign of his neediness. As the party ended, I stumbled outside to meet him, and he launched in to kiss me. He started to bite my tongue. Now, this wasn't a nibble; this was a full-on vampire bite. Ouch!

It hurt. In my typical fashion, I started to find excuses to justify why he was doing that. I came up with, *He's drunk. I'm sure he kisses better when he's sober.* He asked if I wanted to go back to his to listen to him play his guitar. "Can I check, do you play all the strings?" (thinking back to that one-string musician). He gave me the weirdest look but fuck sitting through that one string wonder again. I wasn't ready for the night to end, so we walked to his place. I clung to the hope that maybe he would kiss better when we got back to his.

You would have thought the short walk to his house would have been straightforward. Now I'm not exaggerating when I say he must have asked me about fifteen times on the twenty-minute walk if I was okay. 'Are you okay?' A minute later, 'Janey, are you okay?' I instantly thought of Michael Jackson's song *Smooth Criminal* and was ready to whip out the moves and tell him to 'beat it'. If there was any silence, the question would come again.

Why do people continually ask you why you are okay? According to good old Google, the reasons are:

- It's a symptom of their social anxiety disorder.
- They are narcissistic or have another personality disorder.
- It's the result of a person's inability to empathise with someone else's feelings.
- He or she may not think asking this will make you feel uncomfortable or annoyed.

Lovely, it looked like I was on a date with someone with some type of personality disorder.

Martin kissed me again, and yes, the biting was still there. My face must have said it all after the kiss, because he asked his favourite question again. 'Are you okay?' A major turn-off!

When I arrived at his flat, I asked for some water. 'Are you okay?' was the response. Well, that wasn't going to be stopping anytime soon. He handed me a measuring jug filled with water. No clean mugs or glasses in that kitchen of yours, Martin? Turned out he hadn't done his dishes for a while. Well, if his kitchen wasn't clean, I had to wonder what else wasn't clean.

The night was getting weirder and weirder.

I listened to him play his guitar while I drank from my jug of water, and I kept thinking how his playing would sound if he had kept those extra digits – he could be Instagram famous, for sure.

I started thinking what his stage names could be: Extra Fingers, Two Extra Stubs, I've got it! Martin and the Hula Hoops with his musical style being stub step.

I grabbed a blanket from his couch, as I was starting to feel cold, and he asked if I wanted to share a bath to warm up. Now, Martin had never seen me naked, so what made him think I was going to strip off and work out who was sitting at the tap end at two in the morning?

And that was that … TAXI!

As soon as I had left, my phone pinged. Guess what the message said…

'Are you okay?'

TB Chat

Louise – How did your date go, you on to a winner?
Jane – If a winner is someone who makes you rub their pinky stubs, forgets their PIN, and asks if you are ok a gazillion times then I guess yes!
Senga – Pinky stubs? Need more details
Weejo – I don't know what's worse out of the three
Jane – I might be the first person in history whose date involved rubbing finger stubs

Tips

1. Too much information on the first date can be a mood killer and lead to judgements. Flaws, habits, differences, etc. can all become things a partner will love about you, a first date might be less open-minded/more judgemental.
2. If a date asks, 'Are you okay?' numerous times, then it's not okay to be with them. Google says they are a narcissist or have another type of personality disorder, and Google is always accurate - right?
3. If your date doesn't have any clean mugs/glassware, then you need to question what else isn't clean. You never know what's creeping about down there.

Flash in the pan

My friend had hired a personal trainer called Ethan, and asked if I could come along to a workout session for moral support.

When I approached the PT, I instantly recognised him from a dating app, hello Popeye! I hadn't swiped right because he had his six-pack on display in *every* single picture. I mean, sure it was nice, but I prefer to see a bit of variety in dating app pictures to get an impression of their personality too. You've got to leave some things to the imagination. I feel these types of images indicate the man is too cocky.

I would say I am judgemental - if I see images of a man not smiling, I assume he will be dull and boring. If a profile only has one image, I will always swipe left. As if they don't make an effort with adding two or three pics, then I feel that they are probably lazy and not interesting.

I had arrived from a photoshoot and was absolutely mortified because my hair was bright blue. Even my forehead was stained blue, so I looked like a Smurf. It was too late to turn back though, so I tried to impress him by going for it with the exercises. I could feel my face getting redder and redder while the blue dye ran down my cheeks.

After the class, he asked for my details in case I wanted any more PT sessions in the future. A day later, he messaged to ask if my hair was back to normal. Check him breaking data protection - not very professional.

I still wasn't interested, because personal trainers aren't my type (purely because I like to devour a bag of chocolate buttons a night, a habit I'm more than happy to continue) so I kept it short and sweet and said it would take a few more washes. I thanked him for the PT session and said I would be in touch if I wanted any more.

A few weeks went by and another message appeared on my phone from him. He said he'd not heard from me which he took to mean I didn't want any more sessions. That was good for him, because it meant he could ask me on a date. Was I interested? I really hadn't been expecting him to ask me out on a date. Since I was currently single, I thought, *Why not?* I could at least stare at his bulging biceps during dinner.

Our first date was okay. He was training to be a bodybuilder, so he was ordering healthy food. He ordered plain chicken, salad and a side of green vegetables. I guessed I'd better hold off on ordering a pizza and opted for a salad like him – gutted! When our salads came out, I couldn't help but feel annoyed at myself for not ordering what I really wanted… McDonald's drive-thru was definitely happening on the way home.

He had a competition the following weekend, so we arranged to go on another date once that was out of the way. That way he'd be able to relax and eat some junk food. I couldn't deal with another plate of lettuce.

The second date came around, and we went to Sapporo Teppanyaki restaurant. I thought it was a perfect choice, because it provides entertainment throughout our meal, and the chef throws food into your mouth – always hilarious to watch.

Ethan was quiet throughout the whole meal. Everyone else in the restaurant was laughing at the chefs; I was bent over double at the people who couldn't catch food in their mouth. People were being splatted in the face by potato, what's not to laugh about that.

I asked if he was okay (I want to point out I only asked him one time, nothing like Martin), and he said he was fine though he wasn't feeling great. He suggested we finish the food and leave. I realised he had barely eaten his food; I kept eyeing it up because I was still hungry. If we were a few dates in I would have asked if I could eat the rest of his food but didn't want to seem like a gannet*.

I guessed he must have been feeling upset about not winning the competition. I had thought this restaurant would cheer him up, but it had clearly been a bad decision.

As soon as we got outside the restaurant, Ethan let out an almighty gasp. He was panting heavily, and he sat down on the ground. Oh, my word! *He's having a heart attack* was my first thought. I started to think back to episodes of Grey's Anatomy to work out what the hell I needed to be doing. Think Jane! Think! What would Dr McDreamy do?

He got out his phone and dialled a number. He passed the phone to me, and it said 'Mum' on the screen. Shit, I wasn't ready to speak to his mum; I'd rather have spoken to the ambulance or NHS 24 than his mum. I told his mum that Ethan was showing signs of having a heart attack. Rule number one, don't say that to a mother. She explained that he was having a panic attack, and he had them regularly. She was a nurse, so luckily knew how to resolve the situation.

She asked me to go back to his, make him a cup of tea, and make sure he went to bed. If I could check on him throughout the night and give her an update then that would be great…Eh?

I had no first aid skills so I was worried about being alone with him, especially since I had no experience with someone having a panic attack. I had never even been to his place and now I was being asked to play nurse – and not the kind of nurse one might have hoped to be.

A panic attack is the abrupt onset of intense fear or discomfort that reaches a peak within minutes and includes at least four of the following symptoms:

- Palpitations, pounding heart, or accelerated heart rate.
- Sweating.
- Trembling or shaking.
- Sensations of shortness of breath or smothering.

It was so awkward in the taxi to his place. He was clearly embarrassed. He seemed to be over the worst now. He opened up that he used to have them quite regularly, apparently he used to take too many gym enhancers and this so happened to be one of the side effects.

I followed the request of his mama and made him some herbal tea which is apparently calming. it was then I started to show signs of panic.

Age ten, I sat my hostess exam at Brownies. In order to receive my badge I had to make tea for one of the volunteers. I remember putting the tea bag in the mug, chucking in loads of milk, two heaped teaspoons of sugar, taking the teabag out almost instantly and then I sat back to watch her reaction, a reaction I wish I could unsee. The look of disgust was enough to know I failed at making tea.

I was told to work on my tea-making skills and redo the badge at a later stage. Well, I don't drink tea so I've never practiced and my parents wouldn't ask for tea as they know too well it won't be pleasant.

Still, I handed over the mug to my 'date' and encouraged him to go to bed while I headed to his spare bedroom to avoid seeing his tea disgust reaction. It was weird being inside his home. There was no TV in the spare room, so I lay there in silence. It wasn't even late into the night yet.

I scrolled through my social media, messaged my friends but I was bored and really wanted to go home. I updated his mum to say he was asleep, I secretly wanted to ask her if the pills he used to take have any effect on his testicles. I heard certain enhancers can shrink your balls, she's a nurse so I'm sure she would know or one of her colleagues would.

In the morning, Ethan was acting uncomfortable. I felt bad for the guy – I would have been embarrassed as well. It's not nice to have people witness you going through an experience like that.

I once fainted at primary school at a dress rehearsal for the school show. I remember being so self-conscious about it that I told my mum I was too unwell to do the show.

Ethan never contacted me for another date.

On the plus side, I now know what to do if someone has a panic attack. Always a lesson learned in every situation, although shame I didn't get to see his tiny bawbag*.

TB Chat

Jane – You can now refer to me as Nurse Jane, pretty much saved my date's life
Senga – Please don't tell me your date had a heart attack. Was it an old guy you went on a date with?
Weejo – I'm about to board a plane, tell me quickly
Jane – He had a panic attack and I helped by telling him to breathe slowly
Louise – Therefore, you did not save a life. He will no doubt be too embarrassed to see you again

Tips

1. If you are with someone who is experiencing a panic attack, stay with them. An attack can last between twenty and thirty minutes. Staying with someone provides comfort to them.
2. Stay calm. If you are stressed, it will only make the other person feel more anxious which will make the attack worse.
3. Make conversation and get the person to talk to you – it will distract them from the attack.

Glossary

** Gannet: A person who is always hungry and will eat almost anything, originates from the large seabird that catches fish by plunging into the water*

** Bawbag: Scottish word for scrotum*

How important is four inches after all?

I have found, with some of my friends that we have ended up chatting to the same person online. My advice is to screenshot pics of men you are chatting to so you don't end up speaking to the same hottie. Out of my groups of friends, we have Louise who has the hots for Italians, Weejo who prefers the older man, Senga who likes men with a bald head, Marissa who is into men younger than she is, and Rachael who will only date men who weren't born in the UK as she likes the thought of her future children being bilingual. This last one was the crossover when I got chatting to Jonathan. He didn't live in Scotland; he was German and worked in banking. He regularly had meetings in Glasgow, so we decided to meet next time he flew into the city.

It was when Jonathan added me on Instagram that I noticed my friend followed him. I messaged Rachael and she said he had wanted to meet her, but she wasn't interested anymore because she recently met someone else who she liked – phew! She was keen to hear all about my date with him though, so she could envisage what she would have gone through. That's sometimes the problem with online dating – you can match with the same person your friend/relation/colleague has matched with.

We agreed to meet at a tapas restaurant when he would be in town a few weeks later. By all accounts, this guy was beautiful. His Instagram had lots of pictures of him on his travels, lots of selfies with beautiful sunsets behind him. I was looking forward to getting to know him.

I was working in Dundee that day (eighty miles from Glasgow city centre) so had to pack everything I needed for the date and succumb to getting ready in the train toilet, what luxury! Now as you may be aware, train toilets are not the most pleasant of places to get dolled up in. Normally, they stink of pee or poo, there tends to be urine/water on the floor and the train jerks suddenly – it's a challenge at the best of times.

I wished I had been more organised the night before, why didn't I plan ahead instead of bingeing on Netflix series and then being too lazy to beautify? I'm notorious for only putting tan on a few hours before heading out.

My train routine involved the following: shave my legs, moisturise, apply fake tan, wait ten minutes for the tan to dry, put on my dress, brush my teeth, apply makeup and brush my hair. Apologies to the commuters who were waiting in a queue outside the smelly cubicle, but I wasn't working in the best conditions.

Several times, I stood in the urine on the floor due to the movement of the train and had to baby-wipe my feet. Honestly, I don't understand how I get myself into these situations! I also cut myself while shaving my legs, again thanks to the commotion of the locomotion. I clearly forgot I cut myself until I put the fake tan on and oh my gosh, it fucking stung. My pores were opened so, of course, it would sting, I had clearly forgotten during my mad rush to go from ogre to Princess Fiona. I let out a frustrated scream, "Fuck!" and then, of course, heard a chap on the door.

I exited the toilet with my head down, making sure I made zero eye contact with the queue that had now formed. I was sweating by the time I made my way back to my seat. All I could think was, *This guy had better be worth it!* My legs were a mix of redness and patchy tan. At this point, I had it in my head if I show some cleavage he will be distracted, that he won't care about my now unattractive pins.

On my way to the restaurant, Johnathan messaged to say he was walking there and would be about ten minutes. I replied with a joke, saying *I'll race you... I know you'll win though as you have longer legs.*

It turned out it was me who had the longer legs. Now, I'm not one of those girls who declares she will only date someone of a particular height – I *have* dated guys who were shorter than me. But he was about 5 ft. 3, and with my heeled boots on, I was 5 ft. 7. It was so awkward. I have noticed that short guys will usually mention it online, because they don't want to turn up and have a girl looking down on them. This guy would have been much more suited to my friend Rachael as she is 5 ft.

The thing with his Instagram was that there were no group pictures of him and his mates which would have given away his height...maybe that's why he didn't have those kinds of pictures on there?

His first comment to me was, 'Maybe I should have told you I wasn't blessed in the height department.' Then he told me my leg was bleeding. Dammit! The boobs clearly were too hidden but to be fair, his head was in-line with my thigh, so he couldn't have missed the trickle of blood. Little did he know the pain I had to inflict during dress up from hell?

We *did* have a nice meal and a good catch-up, but we both knew it wouldn't go anywhere, especially when I had to bend down to give him a hug goodbye.

This isn't the only time this has happened to me. I met a guy called Kane at a music festival who was out of this world. In my drunk state, I couldn't quite believe this guy was chatting to me – he was a definite ten out of ten. He looked so gorgeous with his shades, tanned skin, and good taste in fashion. We danced together while the music blared, then he dragged me to the silent disco tent. I couldn't stop laughing and smiling. We swapped numbers and arranged to meet after the festival was over.

Kane and I met up a week later at a TGI Friday's restaurant. Luckily, he lived not too far from me. I turned up at the restaurant, and was actually very excited – I felt it would be a fun date.

Approaching the restaurant, I couldn't see him. I had to look at the picture on my phone to remind myself what he looked like. I can only describe my reaction as one of complete shock. Kane was tiny. He hadn't been tiny at the festival. I didn't understand. He also had a squint eye. Sunglasses can be pretty deceiving. It became clear to me that I'd had my beer goggles on.

I hadn't seen his eyes at the festival because it's perfectly acceptable to wear sunglasses all day and all night at a music event. But how had I not noticed his height? Well, I logged into my Bebo* account (it was a more innocent time before Facebook but after MSN and dial-up internet, how did we survive!), to check my festival pictures and zoomed in on his feet – he was wearing heeled wellies! I didn't even know they existed. Though I had heard Tom Cruise and Simon Cowell wear heeled boots – very deceiving.

More on four inches later!

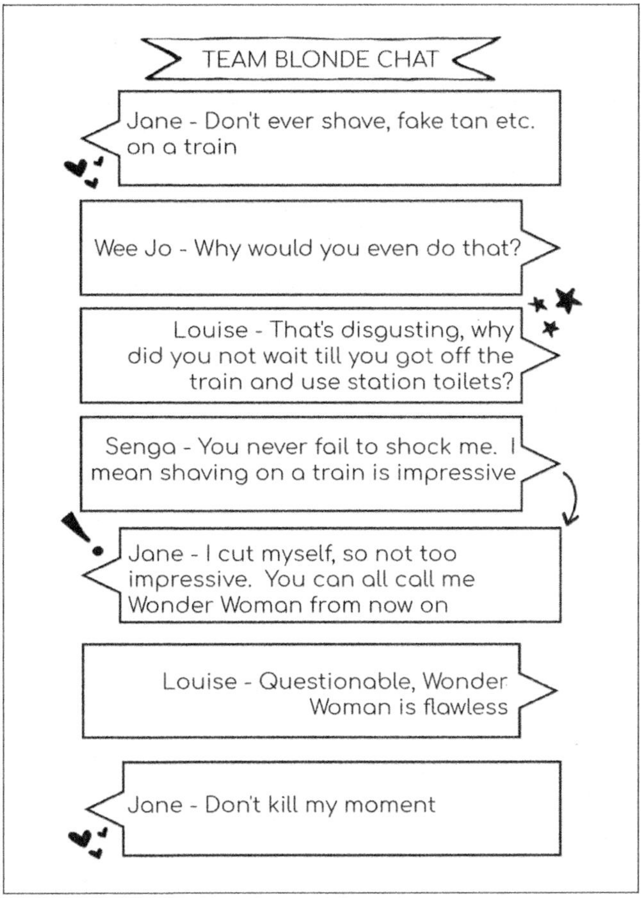

Tips

1. Openly ask what height a potential date is. Be funny and say it's so you know whether to wear flats or heels.
2. If the date adds you on social media beforehand, have a look at group shots. That will give an indication of their height.
3. If you meet someone who is wearing shades at the time, ask them to remove them early on to take in their true identity.

Glossary

** Bebo: the social networking website before Facebook. It was launched in 2005. It overtook Myspace and, at the time, was the most popular social networking site. It was incredible, as a teenager, having this app to chat to boys.*

Sleepers creepers

I am sure we have all experienced falling asleep next to a person who either snores, sleep talks, farts, or pees the bed when they are drunk (I hope this is the minority). But have you experienced someone watching you sleep?

Creepy, right?

Hellooo, Matthew. His profile stood out, because every picture was of him and this gorgeous golden retriever puppy. I was sucked in. Any pics of dogs will melt my heart. A good tactic gentleman, a good tactic indeed.

Matthew was full of positivity. He was a really spiritual person, maybe I needed a bit of that in my life? He saw the good in everyone and was positive about all aspects of life. He didn't believe money made you happy. Instead, he believed that if you were happy in yourself, good things would come your way.

What a nice way to get through life. Here was a man who was creative and got joy from playing music, painting, and listening to his vinyl records.

On our first date, we agreed to take his puppy for a walk. The doggie was hyperactive and adorable. The date was fun. The only thing that spoiled the day was when Matthew told me the puppy wasn't his. It was his brother's. *Funny you forgot to mention that during our chat, it must have slipped your mind.*

He wasn't exactly my type. Sure, he was refreshing to be around, but money not being even a smidge of a priority wasn't for me. I must admit, I work hard so that I can have enough money to buy luxuries or save for a holiday.

When he got his roll-ups out and started making a cigarette, he really lost my interest. Smoking is a no-no for me. I was very aware that I can be overly fussy, and thanks to the mixture of Matthew's positivity and the cute puppy, I let this issue slide.

Matthew talked about how he couldn't wait to raise kids, and how he wanted to have kids sooner rather than later. Okay, calm down – let's have less of that chat at this early stage. He mentioned that, with both of us being creative, we could form a touring band. Eh … no, thanks! I'll pass on that. I don't want to be the next Osmonds or Von Trapp family.

Yet, there was something mesmerising about him. One evening, I went over to his place to hang out, and I don't know if it was the smell of the incense burning, but I passed out on his couch. I woke up and could hear Matthew singing along to his records. I apologised for falling asleep and said I'd best be on my way. Matthew told me it was midnight and I could stay over since the trains had stopped for the night.

He had to be joking! I felt such a mix of emotions. Should I be annoyed that he didn't wake me up? Was it because he had another agenda? I did feel safe around him though, so I got rid of that thought instantly. We hadn't been intimate at that stage, and I didn't want to take it to that level. I said I would crash on the sofa, but he insisted I take his bed, and he would sleep on the couch – very kind of him.

He was walking around in his boxers, and that is when I noticed his bum. It was tiny. One of my thighs was bigger than his whole butt. As awful as it sounds, I wasn't sexually attracted to him. I mean, I don't think I was. He took me through to the bedroom, and as he said goodnight, he leaned in to kiss me. I mean, what harm could come from a kiss?

While we kissed, he began shouting 'oh shit' over and over. He touched my breast – 'oh shit'. He kissed my neck – 'oh shit'. His hand slid up my thigh – 'oh shit'. I was concerned about what would happen if we went all the way. Would he shout 'diarrhoea'?

I told him I wasn't ready to sleep with him. He was understanding and said goodnight then kissed me on the forehead – he didn't shout 'oh shit' this time, just in case you were wondering. As soon as my head hit the pillow, I passed out instantly. Did he have lavender built into his pillows I wonder? The mix of aromas in his house was not conducive to consciousness.

In the middle of the night, I woke to find him staring into my eyes. I got a real fright and Usain bolted upright. Why was he in the bed? Why was he looking at me? I asked him what he was doing. He said he'd got cold and hoped I wouldn't mind. Then he told me he had been staring at me all night, watching me sleep.

This is probably the downside of being a deep sleeper, I can sleep through the full night and rarely wake up to sounds. When I was younger, my bedroom window backed onto the garage which was broken into during the night. My dad had his golf clubs, work tools, etc. stolen and there

I am in my bedroom dreaming of unicorns, oblivious to the noise.

Matthew thought I was beautiful, and wanted to paint me. This was the exact opposite of that scene in Titanic where Kate Winslet sits seductively in the scudder* for Leonardo DiCaprio as he paints her.

Would he paint the drool coming out my mouth or the eye gunk that miraculously appears as if by magic while you sleep? Would he include a speech bubble of my snoring? (Not that I snore, I'm very peaceful when I sleep according to Norman Bates here).

I asked him if he had slept at all. He said he couldn't sleep but felt very peaceful watching me. Instantly, I thought of all the horror movies I had watched. Was this going to turn into a scenario where he trapped me in his flat, never to see the light of day again? The frustrating thing was that my eyelids were getting heavy. I was trying my best to keep my eyes open, so he couldn't watch me sleep again. This guy really needed to lay off these aromas.

My phone battery had died, and I didn't have a charger with me. Matthew used a pay-as-you-go old-school phone, the phone that probably had the game *Snake* still on it, so he certainly didn't have the right kind of charger. This meant I couldn't even set an alarm. I had to rely on waiting for the sunrise to appear for me to know when I could make a run for it.

If only it had been summer and not winter – at least, in summer, the light of hope would have shone through the window quicker.

Spiritual or not, this was way too intense for me. Even now, the smell of sage gives me flashbacks to him.

Thanks, Matthew, for ruining that scent for me.

TB Chat

Jane – Have you ever had someone watch you while you slept?
Weejo – Well, I wouldn't know as I would be asleep
Jane – Hahaha, let me rephrase, have you woken up and realised the guy was staring at you?
Senga – Creepy, who was this?
Louise – Get rid immediately
Jane – Another failed date. Surely statistically I'll meet someone 'normal' soon, right?
Senga – With you? Doubtful

Tips

1. If you catch someone watching you sleep, tell them outright that you are feeling uncomfortable (if you are, no judgement if you're into it).
2. When your sleep-watcher goes to sleep, wake them up while your face is close to them so they get a fright – they might just get the message.
3. Don't fall for the puppy pictures!

Glossary
** Scudder: Scottish word for in the nude*

Don't take the piss

Now, I've heard and read about many of the fetishes out there. They vary from the common and tame ones such as role-play, spanking, and foot fetishes to the more extreme ones such as Regression aka adult babies, Furries aka dress up as animals, and the one I experienced in this story – watersports.

A definition of watersports: A sexual activity that involves urinating on or being urinated on by others. Sometimes referred to as a 'golden shower'. Let me tell you, I wish my experience had been a golden shower. At least then, when the pee hit me, it would have felt like the warm water of the shower.

I had been dating Alan on and off for two years. He was actually the first person I met online. I remember creating my profile and thinking I really didn't want to be meeting someone on the internet.

With my full-time job working in TV production, it was common for me to work overtime. By the weekend, I had no energy to go out. It made meeting men difficult.

Alan was a cheeky character, a flirt, and he had a high sex drive. He hadn't had an easy childhood. He told me he had ADHD, which wasn't diagnosed when he was a kid, so his teachers thought he was badly behaved. As a result, he didn't come out of school with any qualifications, but he was determined and ambitious and did well making money.

Our relationship was fun. He wasn't romantic in the slightest, but he was hilarious and always cracking jokes. Our sex life was ok; he was adventurous and always liked to spice it up but I never felt the romantic passion. I felt like to him it was just sex, not the 'I'm so in love with you' sex.

One night, he told me he had a pee fetish. What? I told him I was definitely not entertaining that. He said all his ex-girlfriends loved being peed on. Surely not? Who were these girls? There was no way that all of them would have liked it. Clearly, he was just telling me this to get me to participate. I refused point-blank. I was not being peed on, end of conversation. I understood people had fetishes - this one was too weird for me.

It became a regular conversation every time we were intimate, '*Go on, let me piss on you*'. My answer remained the same. I looked up watersports online, the first thing you see is porn sites with video headings such as 'Milf pees on stepson', 'Receptionist pees on her boss'. Some of the comments I found on forums from women were that it wasn't that bad, some even enjoyed it. I questioned myself repeatedly, wondering if I should try it once and have it done with. I knew there was no chance I would enjoy it, but relationships are about compromise, right?

The night I told him I was willing to let him pee on me, his face lit up like it was Christmas Day. A big Cheshire-cat grin. I didn't want to do it. Looking back now, I can see I was weak in that relationship. I agreed to go anywhere he wanted to go; I made all the compromises. Deep down, I knew he was cheating on me. Naively, I was trying to prove I was worth being faithful to.

Girls were messaging me, telling me they knew he was cheating on me. Still, I chose to ignore it and tried to convince myself they were jealous. I knew it was true though. I just didn't want to confront him, because I knew that, if I did, the relationship would be over. In hindsight, I can't believe I thought agreeing to be pissed on might save the relationship. I'm gagging now at the memory of it – it was horrific.

The time arrived for my evening at his place, to take a whole different meaning of relaxing in a bath. I was lying in shallow water because he wanted me to feel it all over me. In a sudden moment of clarity, I realised, *I'm about to be pissed on.* Fantasy had turned into reality.

I was doing this for him, not me. What had happened to me? Why had I sunk to this level? The pee came out and the smell and the warmth of it was awful. *Why didn't he drink pints of water during the day so it was clear?* The warmth turned very quickly to cold. I watched him and could tell he was enjoying every second. This was rank* and it made me want to boak*. I felt a sudden change in my personality. At that moment, I decided he wasn't the man for me. There was nothing husband material about what had just happened.

I told Alan that I never wanted to experience that again. In response, he asked me to pee on his face. How degrading would that be? I could picture myself squatting over his face and looking down thinking, *How did our relationship come to this?* Whatever happened to making someone feel special with flowers, dinner...and a bubble bath containing no traces of pee! We had been together for two years. The relationship was coming to a close due to many other factors, but this was the end of the waterfall.

If someone pees on you, it apparently means they want control. He is now married with a child. I wonder, when they put the baby down to sleep, if they have a piss-up – and not the kind involving drinks.

I don't ask for much from relationships. All I want is to be treated with respect and honesty. I often wonder how high-maintenance, fiery women get a man.

Am I choosing the wrong men? Are us nice girls seen as pushovers or boring?

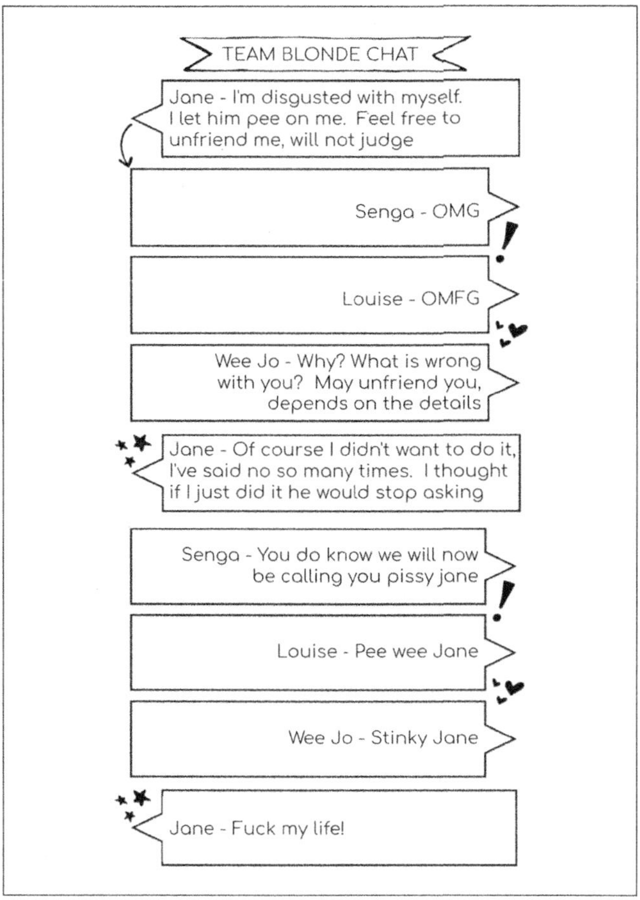

Maybe men secretly like to be bossed about. It's apparently all about the chase, right? My friend once told me that you always need to keep a man on his toes. Well, I can't change my personality, and I don't want to play games.

My top five things a guy could do to make me feel special would be:

1. Compliment me
2. Cook a meal
3. Cuddle up watching a movie
4. Hold my hand
5. Give me little surprises

Simple things. Not over the top or expensive.

My main advice is don't go chasing waterfalls!

Tips

1. If someone wants to pee on you, seriously consider what you are open to and whether you are doing this only for them.
2. You should never feel forced/or talked into doing something you are not interested in. I was trying to save my relationship. What a way to salvage it! Yes, pee on me, and hopefully, it will bring us closer – laughable now.
3. If this is a fetish you are willing to entertain, then perhaps try for the first time in the shower. That way you won't know if it's pee or warm water.

Glossary

** Rank: an offensive odour*

** Boak: Scottish meaning for feeling sick or vomiting*

Master, is it in yet?

I decided to sign up for an evening acting class. I had fallen away from acting and wanted to get my confidence back. I started a beginners' class where the majority of us were all in our twenties. One man, Pierre, was in his late thirties, stylish, French, and a head-turner. I can safely say most of the females and males in the class had a crush on him.

Our teacher gave us a task to concentrate on for the next fortnight. He explained he would put us into pairs, and we had to find a duologue (a script involving two characters) to rehearse outside of class that we would perform in front of the rest of the students. While we waited to hear who our partner was going to be, I was praying not to be paired with Pierre. That would have been mortifying as he always made me blush.

But as fate would have it, he was exactly who I was paired with. Okay, maybe this was meant to be. I need to get on with it, show him I'm confident and comfortable around him. I can do this! I needed to find a script where the characters would have to flirt or, even better, kiss. If I got to kiss him, then I would have fulfilled my desire by using the excuse that it was part of the scene. My research paid off as I found a scene which involved a heated argument that leads to him consoling me. He can add a kiss if he feels it is necessary, which I thought, *I will be 100% encouraging him to do.*

We exchanged numbers and decided on days/times/locations to rehearse. I made more effort with my appearance and clothing. It's funny how this becomes the forefront when you are attracted to someone.

During our first rehearsal, we ended up talking for two hours about our lives. It was clear we were both 'ambitious actors' (we rehearsed three times a week for two weeks). During our rehearsals, he explained he was in a long-distance relationship with a girl in France and said he wanted advice on how to end it with her. *Break up with her and pick me.* No, it would have sounded crazy if I'd blurted that out. I do give good advice though when it comes to other people's relationships. I advised he talked through his issues with her and perhaps they could come to some sort of mutual decision.

Unfortunately, Pierre later pulled out of the performance because he bottled it. No kissy kissy after all. During our time rehearsing, I realised Pierre valued me as a friend, and we ended up becoming good pals. He broke up with his girlfriend, he became more fun and less stressed. We continued to hang out, catching up on our lives.

When I moved to a new apartment, I told him my good news; he knew I had been desperately looking for a new place. He suggested we celebrate my new home at our next catch-up by going for some wine and letting our hair down. Was Pierre flirting with me? On the other hand, was this purely a friend wanting to share my good news? We had now known each other for six months, and there had been no flirting.

The following week, we met for wine, and the flirting began. I was beginning to feel butterflies and didn't know how to act around him. He said he had been attracted to me the first time we started to rehearse for the duologue. I asked why he had never flirted, he said he had been sussing me out to see if I could handle him. Handle him? Does he know who he's dealing with? I'm the girl that has been pissed on, rubbed stubs, and been creepily watched whilst I slept. Bring it on, my little French fancy.

What was it about him that he thought I couldn't handle? When he said we should go back to mine, I instantly felt incredibly nervous. I couldn't believe it – I was going to have sex with the charming French man (another country to tick off, merci). This was going to be incredible. I mean, they do say Frenchmen are great lovers. Time for some ooh la la with Pierre.

Thankfully, I had shaved. Once a guy came back to mine, I was in a predicament as I was due in for a wax the next day. I kept telling him during sex, to not touch or look at me down there, I had grown a bush. The sex wasn't enjoyable at all, I was constantly worried he would catch a glimpse of my new furry friend.

Waxing/shaving is obviously a personal choice. I actually like when a man has some pubes, ideally not a thick spread, it isn't really for me. I feel manscaping is the route men tend to opt for nowadays. I've seen a vast amount of pubic hair on one gent. To look at, I thought it was a turn on, rare to see.

When you're face on with the short and curlies, it's tough. I could only devour half his package as it was a jungle back there. Smelt musky, his balls were not even visible, I could have flossed for days. I was once faced with a set of hairy bollocks which can only be described as looking like a hairy cactus. The man asked me to suck them - suck them I did not. I was either going to be pierced in the face with a sharp hair or cough up a hairball, those aren't chances I'm willing to take.

Back at mine, Pierre started kissing me on my lips, my neck, my shoulders, my ears...he was hitting all the right spots. To my horror though, he asked me to say, 'Thank you, Master.' I burst out laughing. His expression changed instantly to one that told me I was out of line for laughing.

Pierre said, 'Anything I do to you, you need to thank me for after, or you'll be punished.'

Punished?

'Come on, Pierre, just have sex with me. Cut the whole master and sub chat.'

Well, that didn't go down well, he bent me over and started slapping my arse. Holy fuck, that was sore! How do people get pleasure from that? I'm not a fan; my arse was throbbing. When he stopped, I made sure I thanked him.

Now, you see, he hadn't even hinted that he was into this stuff until now. I was caught off-guard. I think most people in that moment would have felt that way. Nevertheless, curiosity did get the better of me. When we eventually got down to it, his body wasn't toned which I hadn't been expecting. *Wow! Those expensive suits he wears must have built-in Spanx.*

I brushed my hand up his thigh to reach for the goods and that's when I noticed he had a very small penis. I hope he's a grower, oh please grow. I'm stroking his erect penis and it's solid like a rock or should I say pebble. It was like a little turtle popping out of its shell to say hello. Was that the reason behind the domination?

I should have known Pierre was too good to be true. It wasn't the passionate sex I had been imagining either. It was below average, not memorable at all. In fact, the only memory I have is his fading handprint on my pink bruised arse. I no longer saw him as the charming Frenchman. I say thank you enough times during the day; I certainly shouldn't have to say it during kissing, foreplay, and sex as well. He said he wanted to take it further next time and try other forms of Dom and Sub play.

I've experienced a role-play fail before so it's probably best for all parties that I declined his offer. A guy I had been sleeping with decided to introduce the good old dress up game. I turned up at his place one evening and he had a leather dress laid out and asked me to put it on. I realised he had got a size smaller than I am, but I was determined to get into it. I pulled at it and stretched it, not letting this smaller size defeat me, and finally, I got it on. I looked in the mirror and realised there was a huge split in the arse; I was mortified. I quickly took it off and said the leather was making my skin itch.

I messaged the girls that night to tell them the story, and it turned out I hadn't ripped it – the arse section was supposed to be like that to provide easy access for the man. To be honest it made me feel good that I hadn't ripped it due to the size, I was quite pleased with myself that I fitted into it after all.

I've also had a date where I thought the guy was introducing role-play but it turned out to be the oddest experience. I swiped a guy who I recognised. It turned out to be an optometrist I went to once before. I explained to him that he gave me a check-up a couple of years back and after a flirty conversation he said he could book me in for an 'emergency' appointment with him. I was loving this, I might be about to kiss, if not shag a guy in his office. It was one of my sex fantasies.

The next day I turned up at his office and the strangest thing happened. He actually took me through a full eye examination. In my head I'm thinking, is he doing role play? Maybe he will place his hand on my thigh as he checks my eyes, yet none of that happened. He even asked me if I experienced any dryness in my eyes. The only thing drying up is my vagina at this stage. I'm questioning how I got this so wrong. Next thing he asks me to read the letters on the back of the door. Should I spell out F U C K O F F?

I begrudgingly read the letters and he said *hmmm I'll have to change your prescription*. The cheeky fuck. Did he see me and decide he wasn't attracted to me? I was baffled. After the examination, he then randomly asked if I felt the vibe he was feeling. Eh what vibe exactly? Any vibe I've got has been killed off with you telling me to stare left, right, then up to the ceiling. I replied that I wasn't sure and he then proceeded to launch towards me to kiss me. I reciprocated but the kiss was awful, he genuinely tongue raped me. He was flicking his tongue so fast like a cat drinks milk. He then starts poking his tongue in out, in out and shaking it all about. I pulled away and he continued to launch in for more.

I said I didn't want to hold up his next patient. As soon as I left the clinic, he texted to say he would love for me to come back in for another 'appointment'. The only appointment I need is with the dentist to check if my tongue hasn't experienced any trauma. Now back to Subs and Doms. Common assumptions about people who participate in BDSM (bondage, discipline, sadism, masochism):

- Those outside of the BDSM community may misunderstand it or see it as people who are psychologically anxious or maladjusted.
- Many believe Doms are looking for a form of control.
- Some people think that BDSM is all about the Dom having control over someone else and see that as exciting. But there should be trust and respect on both sides (and a safe word).

Those were not things I was willing to explore. I don't want to be with someone who wants to control me. Thank you one last time, and goodbye.

TB Chat

Jane – My arse hurts
Senga – Anal
Jane – Ewww no
Louise – I take it he slapped your arse?
Jane – I had to say thank you to him after he slapped my arse, imagine having to do that?
Weejo – Why the hell would you thank him for that?
Jane – If I didn't, he would continue to slap my arse
Senga – You should start charging these men you meet, new profession for you

Tips

1. Before getting involved in BDSM, make sure you talk it through with your partner. Communication is key.
2. If you want to experiment, talk about mutual interests. Don't do anything you feel uncomfortable with.
3. Always have a safe word so the Dominant knows when to stop if you are feeling uncomfortable.

Slip and slide but no ride

I had been working as a researcher for a TV production company. It was the wrap party for a show we had finished working on, aka everyone gets blind drunk because you've worked so hard that you've basically sold your soul to the devil. After the wrap party, a few of us went back to a colleague's house for drinks. It was there I got chatting to one of the editors, Colin. He was very shy, an introvert. He barely made eye contact with anyone. Editors do tend to sit alone in a dark room all day. He was a stereotype of someone in that profession.

As the night went on, I got drunker and drunker. I noticed Colin was on his own, and I felt sorry for him. I made it my mission to interrogate him and get him drunk. I stumbled across to Colin and introduced myself. At this stage, I purely wanted to make him feel comfortable at the party.

Up-close, I realised he was cute. He wasn't my usual type, but we shared passions for snowboarding and travelling. Colin and I exchanged numbers and began meeting up on a regular basis. I saw him only as a friend; I didn't feel any sexual chemistry towards him initially. The more we met up and spent time together, the more I was becoming attracted to him. I find it fascinating how that can happen. You have no initial attraction to a person, then – Boom! Out of nowhere, you see them in a completely different light.

Colin was geeky, intelligent, and shy. We were polar opposites, but as the old saying goes, opposites attract. One night, after a few too many glasses of wine (I really should stop drinking wine as I make far too many bad decisions on that stuff), we started to kiss. Colin was an incredible kisser. He was passionate, brushed his hand against my hair, and told me how beautiful I was. He went all coy and asked if I had ever squirted. I genuinely didn't even know what that was.

Squirting is also known as female ejaculation. A watery liquid comes from the female prostate glands and comes out of the same hole you pee out of. Colin explained that he could do this to me, so I was up for being his guinea pig. I was slightly apprehensive considering my last pee experience, who could blame me. This was completely different though, Colin explained it was going to be a pleasurable experience for me.

A minute later, I'm ready to pee myself. I'm shouting at him to stop as the last thing I want to do is piss* his bed, and he calmly tells me to let go, assuring me it won't be pee. My thoughts were that I should place a bet with him on that one and earn some money while I was on the date.

A second later, I let go and a waterfall came out of me. I was cringing at the sensation of warm water flooding out of me; it even splashed on my face due to the way he was moving his fingers. It felt amazing to let go, but I was freaking out. I looked at him and he said, "Congratulations on your first squirt." Holy shit, I didn't pee myself! Should I high five him? Who was this guy? What else could I learn?

The next time I arranged to go to his, I was excited and thought it would be handy to bring a litre of water with me to replace the fluids that would be pouring out of me. Colin said he wanted to try something else with me. Eventually, he blurted out that he had certain fantasies and asked if I wanted to participate.

Oh no, here we go again, I thought. *I swear, if he pees on me or tries to make me call him Master, I'm giving up on dating.* Where were all the normal men? Did I seriously fuck up in a past life? Was I being punished? They make it look so easy in fairy-tale movies, but in reality, it's like *Mission Impossible.*

Despite my fears, I was intrigued to find out more about Colin's fantasy. He said it was difficult to explain, so it would be easier to show me an example through the medium of porn. I took a deep breath and looked up at his TV screen where I saw a couple covering their *whole bodies* in massage oil. *Ah! Okay, that's not bad at all,* I thought … until the sliding began.

The couple on the screen slid up and down each other, not having sex, just sliding, like when you were a kid and put washing-up liquid on a mat and slid along it for fun…except this was the adult version.

I couldn't understand how he could find it so erotic. Slippery sex would be fun, but for him, it was just about having me lie face down so he could slide up and down my back. No sex. Just sliding. I thought, *Jeez, this is so weird.* What did I do though? Of course, I gave it a go.

Colin removed his clothing and was fully erect. This was my first time seeing his penis, it was angry looking. The head of his penis was purple, so purple it almost looked bruised.

I tried my best not to stare. I wished time would freeze for a few seconds, so I could take a picture of it to send to my friends for collaborative dick analysis.

For your information:

According to medicalnewstoday.com 'The most common cause of a man's penis turning purple is when the glands and blood vessels react to arousal'.

After doing some research later, I came across a few articles and found out there are apparently up to twenty different penis types. I wonder how many types I've seen.

- Sausage which is average length and girth - it's referred to as the most common one
- Banana is curved upward (my favourite as it hits all the right spots)
- Hammer which is a narrow base with a larger head like a mushroom
- Gherkin which is smaller than average in length and girth (seen a few of those)
- Pencil which is long and thin
- Salami, the penis you normally see in porn which is bigger than average (you'll hear more about the salami in another chapter)
- Veiny which doesn't need a description

He asked if I was ready to feel relaxed and helped the process along by giving me a full-body massage. To this day, it is still the most incredible massage I've ever had. It was down to a combination of the generous amount of oil he poured over my back, his hand motion, and the spot-on pressure. I was willing to put aside my reservations about his fetish in exchange for this delightful massage that I didn't even have to pay in excess of forty quid for.

I then felt loads of essential oil being poured all over my body. *He better not get any in my hair.* He got off me for a second, was this to build anticipation for what was about to happen, was he staring at my nakedness bathing in oil? I did think for a second, *I hope he isn't taking a runny**.

I could picture him sliding on me, not being able to stop and ending up in front of me as his whole body eclipsed mine with a bird's eye view of his crown jewels. Then the sliding began. He was literally getting off by sliding up and down my back. I could hear him making these groaning noises – it was well weird. I had to try so hard not to laugh. But I was so relaxed, I was happy to let him go for it – at least, it would make a good story to tell the girls.

Now, in my defence, those of you who have been for a massage will understand how difficult it is to move when the therapist declares the session has ended. You feel sleepy, a dead weight, and all you want to do is stay where you are, not wanting to let go of the relaxed feeling you are experiencing.

While he was sliding away, watching his porn of another man sliding on his partner at the same time, it made me think about all the escorts out there who make decent money without ever even having to have sex. Round of applause to them. I can imagine the agency calling up saying, 'Fancy a full-body massage, no sex, just a man sliding up your back?' Sign me up! Make him a regular!

His groaning got louder, and I suddenly felt a spurt of liquid that I knew wasn't essential oil. On the plus side, my back was well and truly moisturised. He stood up, thanked me for participating and said he was off for a shower. I've always been told it's best to avoid a shower after a massage in order for the oils to settle, but the addition of his own 'oil' at the very end ruined that notion.

After my shower, I made my excuses to leave and the phase-out operation began.

One time, after this escapade, I was getting a massage, and I laughed out loud in the middle of my treatment, remembering Colin sliding up and down on my back. The masseuse must have thought I was a right oddball.

'Never judge a book by its cover' is the motto that springs to mind for this occasion.

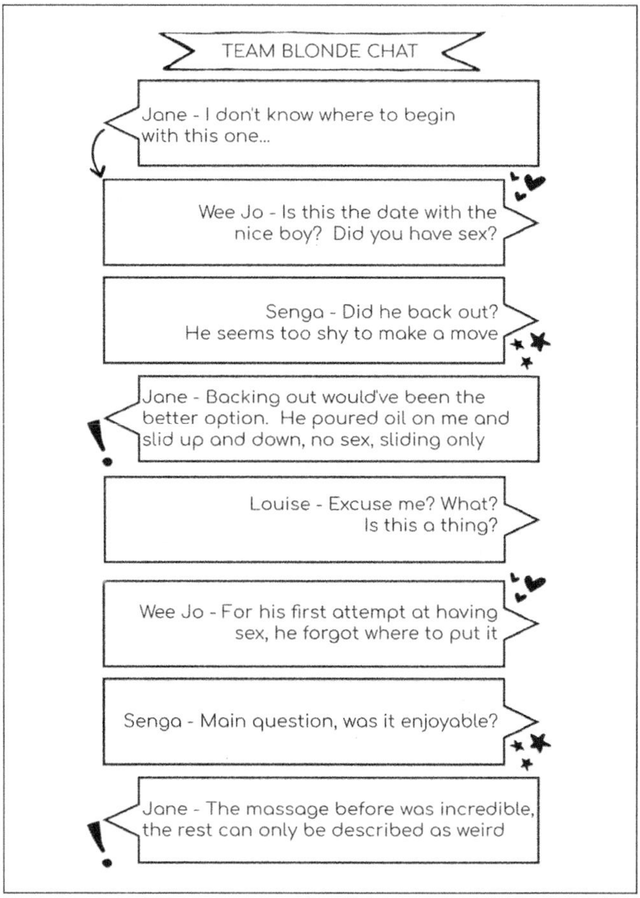

Glossary

** Piss: Scottish word for urine*

** Runny: term used when you were about to take a big run on the slip and slide*

Tips

1. If your partner has a fetish, you need to have an honest discussion about whether you want to entertain it. Some fetishes are best left to the imagination.
2. Your partner is perhaps more likely to entertain a fetish if you are heading into a healthy relationship. If you want to bring it up early on, you could make a joke about it. This way you can see how your partner reacts. If it's positive then you can suggest exploring it.
3. If the sliding fetish is a turn-on for you, I recommend a scented massage oil – that way your partner will be left feeling relaxed and smelling fabulous.

Gone with the wind

I think it's time to return to some stories about the men who made it past the first date. I went out for drinks with Raymond after speaking online for a few weeks. He came across as quite shy during the date, but the chat went well regardless.

Raymond worked as a PE teacher, we talked about sports, which I enjoy watching and participating in (with the minor exception of 'watersports' for obvious reasons). The conversation flowed nicely.

During the evening, an awful stench wafted up my nostrils. It smelt like someone had left a dirty nappy next to us or had simply squatted down and taken a shit right at our table. It was such an overpowering smell that you couldn't ignore it. I had to comment, saying while laughing, that someone had definitely shat themselves. The smell just wouldn't go. It was getting embarrassing. Every twenty minutes or so, the smell would reappear, and I didn't want him to think it was me. He even commented, saying someone must have had a curry last night. A curry would have been mild in comparison – this was toxic!

Eventually, I suggested we move seats because the smell wasn't going away. We moved over to the couch area in the bar, and sure enough, the smell was there too. I started to think it might be him. This time, I didn't say anything. I just spoke through the smell which honestly made me want to gag. It had to be him, but why wasn't he holding it in? After a while, he got up to go to the toilet and was away for about twenty minutes. I hoped that he was doing a poo and putting an end to that smell once and for all. When he returned, he said he'd met someone he knew in the toilets, and that's why he'd taken so long. Cut the crap (excuse the pun) I know you were dropping your load.

Funnily enough, the smell didn't reappear after he returned from the toilet. He asked me if I wanted to meet for another date. Now, you would think his smelly arse would have put me off, but I always believe people deserve a second chance depending on the circumstances. I mean, maybe he got unlucky and the bad flatulence was the fault of a recent meal – how mortifying for him. I was also very aware that I wasn't getting any younger and nobody is perfect, so I might have to suffer the occasional aroma of manure in the pursuit of good chat.

We arranged the next date for the following week. He said he would cook me a meal at his place. A man who could cook – amazing! A tick in the box ... I just hoped it wasn't going to be curry!

The following week, I arrived at his flat. I could smell the food cooking away and it smelt great. When I walked into his place, he leaned in to give me a kiss, and the poogate situation from the first date was all forgiven. But not for long.

I waited in the living room while he finished off the cooking, and I heard about four loud and proud farts. He must have thought I wouldn't be able to hear them. This guy clearly had a farting problem. He was probably trying to get them all out before he brought the food through. All I could think was: *Here you are, Madam – poo-scented lasagne.*

I messaged a friend, and she told me to make my excuses and leave, but I'm not the type of person to do that. I would just have to bear with it and not agree to another date.

Fun fart facts:

- Most people fart between fourteen and twenty-three times per day.
- Most farts are odourless and relatively undetectable.
- It's common for people to feel as though they fart more than others but that's usually untrue.

It looked like I was getting the tail end of his daily allowance. We should have had a morning date. Anyway, out came the food and it was delicious. He put on a movie after we finished eating, and suddenly, the same smell from the first date reappeared. Should I pretend I couldn't smell it? Should I acknowledge it and laugh? What should I do? Help! I was stuck in a cloud of bad gas!

Well, he didn't say anything, and I didn't say anything – typical people-pleasing behaviour. So, there we were cuddled up in a cloud of shit. It took an eternity for the smell to disappear. I couldn't believe he hadn't acknowledged it. He knew I was inhaling his poo particles. We were both sitting there in silence, pretending the bad smell wasn't there.

As soon as the movie was over, he suggested we get comfortable in the bedroom. Was he for real? Did he have no manners? After letting off all that gas, he needed to scrub his arse crack under a hot shower.

Besides, we hadn't even flirted during the movie. All I had been able to think about was when the next whiff of poop would appear. The released smell of shit that would escape when he removed his clothes was not a risk I was willing to take. I could imagine sirens going off accompanied by an automated voice shouting, WARNING! WARNING! EXTERMINATE!

My friend who will remain nameless said she held in a fart the whole night and was so pleased with herself until she fell asleep and woke up to the sound of a foghorn. She had indeed farted so loudly it woke her up but also the man she was in bed with. The fart blasted off his leg, her arse muscles must have got too relaxed throughout the night.

She said she lay there pretending she was still asleep whilst he got up to go to the toilet. As he was away, she said she was wafting the quilt to get rid of the smell and when she 'pretended' to wake up nothing was said. She didn't see him again as she was too mortified about what happened.

She does have tips for us ladies (I mean not that we do it, of course, cough cough).

Below are some tips to avoid this scenario:

1. Wear clothing to bed and stuff your bum cheeks with fabric so if you do fart it softens the blow
2. Drink peppermint tea, it's great for helping your digestive system
3. Don't lie on your belly, more likely to let one slip out due to the pressure on your bowels.

Anyways back to the crap flat, I made my excuses to leave; this was not a guy I wanted to see again. The whiff of fresh Scottish air has never been more appreciated. Thank you, Scotland!

Date number two was definitely a number two in more than name.

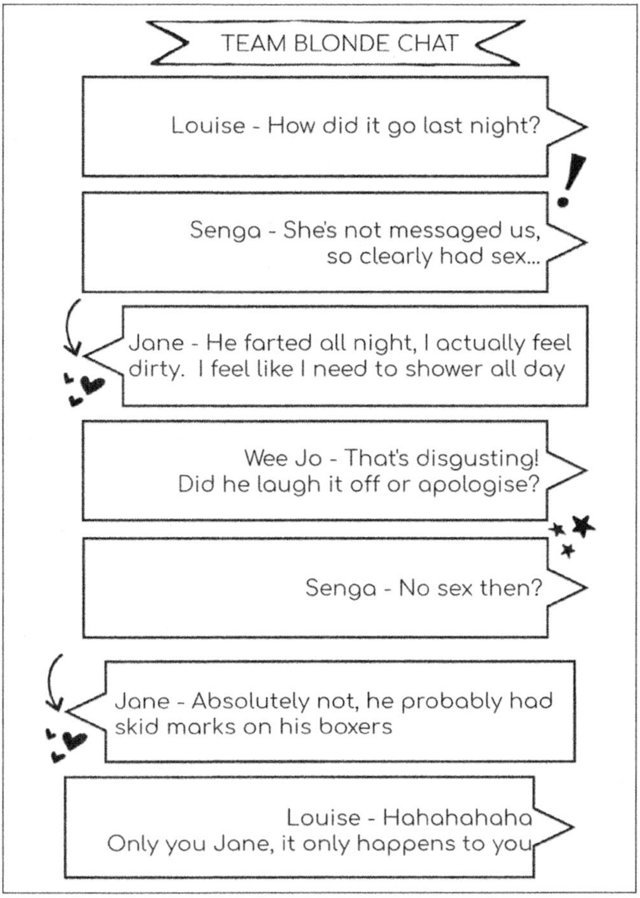

Here is a list of excuses to help you get out of an unpleasant situation:

- Sore stomach
- On your period (some men get awkward when you mention menstruation)
- Urinary tract infection (UTI)
- You've put on fake tan and don't want it to streak
- Tired (most common excuse)
- Bloated (good one if you've recently had dinner)
- Feeling generally unwell

- Headache (another common excuse)
- Not showered so you would rather leave it to another day
- Not shaved so you don't feel comfortable

Tips

1. If you feel like you need to fart, hold that bad boy in, put up with the bad cramps or head to the toilet. No one is going to feel romantic while smelling shit.
2. There are certain foods that can cause flatulence such as onions, beans, broccoli, potatoes, and the ever so popular curry – best to avoid them if you're going on a date.
3. Take probiotics. They can help balance the bacteria in your digestive system.

Service with a smiler

Nowadays, apps are more developed, so you can answer a list of questions that make it easier to communicate your preferences. The app splits what you are looking for into a list of 'dating', 'relationship' or 'not sure'. It also prompts you to answer questions about things like kids, religion, and your political views which ensures less time is wasted. I appreciate those kinds of questions. For example, I won't match with a person who declares he doesn't want kids. It makes the whole process so much smoother.

One man I wasn't attracted to explained on his bio that he could impersonate an air siren. I wanted to match him purely to witness this. Picture the scene, in his car and he sticks his head out the window to act like Harry in the movie *Harry and the Hendersons*, imagine the cars pulling over. Another profile said he could put his full fist in his mouth, all this talent that I could be viewing, if only I got the fanny flutters for them.

Anyway, on to Adrian who I met at my gym. He had an incredible smile and was always very welcoming and friendly whenever I saw him. We decided to go for a sauna and steam after our workout. Well, we now know what each other's bodies look like, and I must say, Adrian had got great results from working out – Oh, my! He had abs, muscly thighs …

Meanwhile, I was lying down at every opportunity to avoid him seeing my roll of stomach fat. Sitting in the sauna one day (he was sitting, I was lying down to stretch out my stomach), he asked if I wanted to hang out outside of the gym – result!

He had recently moved apartments and wanted to go to IKEA to pick up some furniture, so our first date ended up being a walk around IKEA. Now, I'm one of those people who is not a fan of this place. I don't like DIY, I'm terrible at making interior design decisions, and it takes forever to get out of there; it is honestly like a labyrinth.

On this occasion, I have to say I loved it – I think the promise of meatballs had a lot to do with it. It wasn't your typical date, but once we'd got our food and pick 'n' mix, we settled back at his to watch a movie. The day was a success.

The next date we went to a Mexican restaurant. When we met, he hugged me and told me that, as much as he wanted to kiss me, he couldn't because he had a cold sore. Cold sore, *indeed*! Ooft, the size of it on his lip. My friend regularly gets cold sores when she is stressed, and she said she would never go on a date if she had a flare-up.

All I kept focusing on was his lip. But I didn't want to be shallow. The first date had gone well, and I was sure he, his cold sore, and I would have a lovely meal for our second date. I wondered if moving house was stressing him out.

Despite my resolve, I couldn't help staring at it throughout the meal, praying his scab wouldn't fall off into the sharing platter. The size of it on his lip, his face could have charged it rent. His cold sore reminded me of the scene in Austin Power's movie with the guy with the mole and you can't help but stare. I wanted to repeatedly say cold sore, cold sore, cold sore and now I'm being put off my guacaMOLE.

The third date arrived, and he asked me if I would like to come to his. I prayed his lip would be back to normal, and hoorah, it was. We kissed, and we went to the bedroom, however, no joking aside it was like going to bed with a clown. Adrian would not stop smiling. It was so extreme I wondered if his grinning was hurting his jaw.

I once worked at Butlin's* in Skegness where it was important to smile all day in front of the customers. I remember having an aching jaw from showing my pearly whites for a whole shift. Adrian's smiling was a complete turn-off. It wasn't a cute smile; it was creepy. I mean, bless him, he obviously wasn't trying to look creepy, but I want a guy to look deep into my eyes with a sultry look and kiss me passionately.

I turned my head because his smiling was putting me off so much, and he actually said, 'Look in my eyes; I want to see your face.' I looked at him, and his smile was still there, so I closed my eyes hoping his smile would go away eventually. 'Look at me, you're so gorgeous,' he said. Nooooo, the smile was still there. Why wouldn't it disappear? I tried giving him a smile, but that just made his smile get even bigger – I didn't think that was possible.

Note to self: Do not smile at him.

I wondered, if I looked sad, would his expression change? Was this like facial charades? Maybe if I changed position so I couldn't see his face I could get more into it?

If he'd gave me a thumbs up during sex, I wouldn't have been surprised.

Then he started laughing and shouting, 'Yes, yes, yes!' In my head, I was screaming, 'No. No. No!' After his final yes, he lay there smiling. I lay there in shock.

Unfortunately, the whole smiling experience put me off. I have to admit it – I am shallow, and I can't help it! I can see myself ending up alone. I made my excuses the next time he asked to meet. I also had to start going to the gym at a different time to avoid bumping into him.

On a positive note, Adrian met a girl soon after me, got engaged and emigrated to sunny Australia. I feel like I did him a favour by cutting contact, otherwise he wouldn't have met the love of his life – I wonder if she's a smiler too.

At least when they have a cute picture together, she'll never have to ask him to say cheese and their wedding pictures won't need a flash.

TB Chat

Jane – I've turned into a shallow person
Senga – This we already knew
Weejo – You definitely can't be too picky. Maybe that's why you have bad luck with guys?
Louise – What did Adrian do? I thought you liked him?
Jane – He smiles during sex
Weejo – Surely that's a good thing, shows he's having a good time
Senga – Hmmm yeah that's weird. Was it constantly or just as he came?
Jane – Aaaaaaall the time, it was like having sex with the joker but without the clown face

Tips

1. If the person you are getting it on with does something that is a turn-off, suggest things that turn you on. Hopefully, they will do more of the turn-on than the turn-off.
2. If you have a cold sore, black eye, rash, bloodshot eye, or any other short-term body issue then probably best to postpone the date, first impressions are important.
3. If you like the person but the sex is not up to scratch or improving with suggestions you offer, perhaps it's time to let them go. Sex is an important part of a relationship (for most), and you can't be compatible with every partner you meet.

** Butlin's: a chain of affordable family seaside resorts in the UK providing entertainment and well known for its Redcoats who host and organise activities.*

On the hunt for...

My flatmate told me about a guy he met briefly at a friend's party and thought we would get on great. He described Jeremy as hard-working, funny and up for a laugh. He showed me a picture and I thought the guy was cute. My number was passed on and a date was arranged.

He was in the army and had been away for a few months, so he was desperate to meet at a bar for a pint. I was going through a non-drinking phase but said I was more than happy to meet at a bar to get to know each other. When I arrived, he hugged me and his opening line was, 'This bar is full of cunts, but it will do for now.'

Cunts? Did he actually say that word? They say you will know within ten seconds if you are attracted to someone. Well, this guy broke it within five seconds. My thoughts summed him up as a C U Next Tuesday. I understand that it can be nerve-racking meeting someone for the first time, so I smiled and thought I would let it slide. As the conversation was flowing, he mentioned on more than one occasion that he had appeared on a TV show and wanted to show me a few clips. It was very cringe, but this was clearly his pride and joy. In the dating programme, he came across as really cocky. If only he had sent me it before the date – I would have cancelled and not wasted my time. My sensible head told me not to judge. Perhaps he had changed since the recording. I mean, maybe he was just acting that way for the cameras.

I wanted to find out more about his career. I thought it must be tough being in the army. He told me fascinating stories about his work life. I would have given anything to have a clicker counter because he must have said the C-word over fifty times. He used it like any other casual word. Cunt cunt cunty cunt.

'Me and all the other c$&*! were getting ready to attack.' 'All the c$&*! in the army are easy to get on with.' 'I'm a total c$&*! as I didn't want to join the army.' 'It was my birthday a few weeks back, and the lads pulled a belter* of a prank on me – honestly, utter c$&*!.'

Four pints down for him and two soft drinks for me, I was ready to call it a night when he sprung it on me that his dad was dying. Nooooooo! Do not do this to me. I couldn't deal with that kind of chat with someone I barely knew. I thought, *Maybe this explains the excessive drinking and the bad language.* He was clearly hurting and wanted someone to talk to.

The mood changed and I felt drained, he was the definition of a fun sponge*. The date was awful. I felt I had turned into a therapist. I decided I needed an excuse to leave. I said I was going to call it a night as I was starving. As soon as I said it, I knew I should have thought of a better excuse, because he said they served food at the bar. He'd order me some grub, and we could call it a night after that. I handed him over a £20 note and he went to the bar to order my small starter. He came back with a pint (no doubt with my money) and continued his conversation. *Where's my change?* I thought. It was a £4 starter. He'd kept my change, and yes, he really was a c$&*! Not only was I drained (and my purse), I was annoyed and wanted to leave.

My two chicken satay skewers arrived. As I started eating one, he grabbed the other one and ate it. He didn't even ask. I could feel the anger erupting. I'm like Joey from Friends and don't like to share food. I basically paid £20 for one satay stick. I should have spoken up and asked for the change, but I was genuinely speechless and his dying dad situation didn't help. That was the most expensive satay stick that I have ever eaten, and it didn't even taste that good.

He was now on his sixth pint. I mentioned that I had to go because I had to be up early in the morning. He downed his pint and asked if he could get a lift home. By this point, I had had enough.

I lied and said I was sorry, but I was going to my sister's first to pick something up. He said it was cool and he'd just wait in the car. *No, you bloody well won't.* I explained I wasn't sure how long I'd be at my sister's, so it would be best for him to make his own way back. He finally took the hint and said he would get a taxi. I have never been so relieved to get away from a date.

The first thing I did was text my mate saying, 'You are a total cunt'.

Etiquette on a First Date:

Do

- compliment each other.
- engage in light and friendly conversation.
- talk about your hobbies and interests.

- wear something pleasing to the eye that you'll feel great in.
- tread carefully around certain subjects like relationships and what you are looking for.
- be polite.
- if the date went well, don't be worried about saying you would like to meet again.
- end the date with a hug or a kiss.

Don't

- over compliment, too much can be off-putting.
- moan about your life or tell your date your life issues.
- slag off the other person if their interests are different.
- wear something creased, over the top, or dirty.
- tell them you are looking for a husband/wife and kids on the first date. That would scare anyone away.
- swear or be offensive.
- wait till the date is over and play a guessing game about who will message first.
- be too tactile – it's all about the flirt and the tease.

TB Chat

Weejo – How did the blind date go?
Jane – He said the c word about a gazillion times, just casually saying it repeatedly as if it was a normal thing to do. He technically also stole from me!
Louise – Swearing is very unattractive, especially that word.
Weejo – Did you call him a cunt to his face?
Jane – No because his dad is dying, it was a draining date
Senga – I love that word, such a funny word isn't it? Poor Jane!

Tips

1. If it is a friend who has set you up, find out as much information from them as you can. It turned out my mate barely knew him.
2. If you are not drinking, I would recommend not meeting at a bar.
3. If the chat becomes sombre, change the subject straight away.

Glossary

** Belter: Scottish word for outstanding*

** Fun sponge: a person who is humourless and sucks away any fun*

Dr Junior will see you now

Amir worked as a gynaecologist, a very interesting job. We met online and had our first date at Anchor Line cocktail bar in Glasgow. He had these gorgeous brown eyes that would undress me with each sultry look; they were hypnotic. I was staying with relatives that night so planned to only stay out until midnight.

The thing about Amir was he was the type of person you wanted to stay out all evening with. He was silly, had a great sense of humour…and those eyes. His line that got me weak was, 'All I can think about is kissing you right now.' *Go for it, Amir; you can plant those luscious lips on me all night.* We were acting like teenagers, snogging all night in the bar. It was bloody brilliant.

He asked me to come back to his place, but I wanted to treat him mean and keep him keen. I explained that I wouldn't go back to someone's home on the first date, and he said he understood. It doesn't sit well with me when a man you like wants you to go back to his on the first date; there's no real way to know if he's only wanting sex. I'd learned that the hard way when I was younger.

It makes me want to bring out the dating app and point to their bio where it states they are looking for a relationship. If that's the case, why are they making it feel like a booty call? A few of my male friends say they like to have sex as soon as possible in case the sex isn't up to scratch. That way they don't waste their time wining and dining only to be disappointed. It's a shame how this seems to be the way the future of relationships are heading.

Amir messaged me the next morning saying he was intrigued to find out more about me and that he had really enjoyed my company. I was unsure what to do; I really didn't want it to be all about sex. My friends encouraged me. They thought he'd probably rate very high in the bedroom department since he dealt with vaginas all day. For research purposes, it seemed only fair to be able to report back to my friends on his bedroom abilities. I mean, who knows female anatomy better than a gynaecologist.

I arrived at his apartment, and it was spotless. A man who can look after himself – tick in the box. His cooking was delicious – another boxed ticked. And he really did make an effort with his outfit – tick, tick, tick.

During our conversation over dinner, he sprung it upon me that he had two kids and an ex-wife and didn't want to get married or have kids again. Wow, that was a lot of information to take in. *Here I go again!*

Please mention these specifics on your bio. There are plenty of women who have kids and want to meet a man who also has kids, there are also women who don't want kids and are more than happy to date a man with kids. I *did* want kids, so I already knew this date had no potential. So, the only option was to make it a booty call. He asked how I felt about him having kids. We had an adult conversation and both agreed it was not going to work. The thing is, we were very sexually attracted to each other.

He leaned forward to kiss me, lifted me up and took me to the bedroom. Now, I don't know how anyone else feels about being carried, but I actually hate it. Will he be thinking, 'Wow, she's heavier than I thought?' *Is he going to pull a muscle? Can he see my rolls of fat hanging out?* – It's not pleasant

He carried me into his bedroom, and the foreplay began. Amir asked me not to give him a blowjob, as he didn't like them. Didn't like them? My first thought was I can't wait to tell my friends this news as a few of my friends dislike giving todgers a suck. When sucking a guy off, your mind can wander, especially if the guy doesn't seem close. And if the man is drunk, it can take even longer. Sometimes, there isn't even any point taking on the task if he is six beers plus down.

I often wonder what men think us ladies are thinking about when we have our mouth wrapped around their weapon.

Here are some examples:

1. My jaw is starting to hurt.
2. Eww his balls are so hairy.
3. His toes arch when I'm sucking him, interesting.
4. What will I make for dinner?
5. He better not unexpectedly cum in my mouth.
6. What present should I get for Gary and Heather's wedding?
7. He makes the most unusual noise, it's kind of annoying.
8. Why is this taking forever? Hurry up and cum.
9. His dick is too big for me to even enjoy this, this really is a job.
10. His wee man is so small, this is the easiest blowjob of all time.
11. Why the fuck is he grabbing my hair and pushing his penis more in my mouth, does he want me to choke?

12. Stop asking me to look at you when I'm doing this, why do men like that, it's weird.
13. He's getting close and I'm getting exhausted, I want to switch my hand but this will set the whole process back.
14. I wish I had a hair bobble.
15. Can't believe he's just came in my hair, fuck sake!
16. How many calories does semen have?
17. Lovely, cum all over my boobs. It feels disgusting.
18. Can't believe he's asking me to swallow, you try swallowing three teaspoons of your cum.
19. I wish I could take a pic of his cum face, it's so funny.
20. He's not going to want sex now that he's came.

Now when I was writing this list, it got me thinking. What do men think when going down on a female? Well the wait is over ladies, here are some replies I got from my male friends:

1. I hope she doesn't smell down there.
2. Her flaps are so big, I can wear them as a mask.
3. She's too hairy, her pubes are going in my mouth.
4. There is a musky smell.
5. It's like a waterfall down here.
6. Is that toilet paper residue on her vagina?
7. Yes! She's groaning, I'm a pro at this.
8. What's with the orders, I've gone left, right, up and down, so demanding. Never going to be able to listen to my Sat Nav again.
9. My neck is starting to hurt, I hope she cums soon.
10. Was that a real orgasm or a fake one?
11. My tongue is tired, I'm going to finger instead.
12. Tastes quite tangy.
13. Her asshole is resting on my nose which is kind of filthy. I love it.

14. I can't breathe when you're pushing my face on your clit.
15. Please don't fart on my face.
16. She wants me to play with her breasts as well, I can't multi-task.
17. My face is going to smell of vagina, wonder if she will still kiss me.
18. Can we have sex now?
19. I think she's just came, how long do I wait before I can put my dick inside her.
20. If there was an Olympic sport for this, I would definitely win.

Now back to Amir, the next part of the foreplay was very strange. He didn't touch or even look at my vagina once. If he was put in front of a line-up of vaginas, I can promise you, he would not know which one was mine. Who doesn't touch a vagina? Had his job scarred him?

Amir spent the majority of his time playing with my boobs, and I felt like I was turning into a man trying to get him to move his hand southwards… Nope, every time I tried, it slid back up to my nipples.

Had he seen so many vaginas at work that they were no longer a sexual object to him? Had he fixed botched vaginas so now he pictured mutated ones whenever he saw one?

I was thinking, *I had bet Amir was going to be amazing at foreplay since he uses his hands all day and knows the ins and outs of vaginas, but this is just a huge disappointment.*

No climax, all anti-climax.

Now, if you think that was weird, then it only got weirder. He put on this childlike voice and said, 'Junior is all ready for you.'

Junior? Hahahahaha! He did not just say that? I actually laughed, which he was not happy about. He said, 'Come on, let's take this seriously.'

Seriously? You're naming your bits the first time we are about to have sex? Don't get me started on the creepy voice.

This took me back to the movie, *How to Lose a Guy in 10 Days*, when the lead, Kate Hudson, names the guy's manhood Princess Sophia, in order to put him off her. Matthew McConaughey who is the man in question recommends calling his shlong Krull, the warrior king.

I spoke to a few friends to see if they call the male anatomy a particular name, it got us chatting about the funny names we have heard for male genitals.

- Disco stick, anaconda, pee-wee, chopper, winkle, piece, fire hose, pink cigar, hot rod, weapon, Johnson, spitstick, love truncheon, one-eyed trouser snake, unit, donkey kong, chopper, weeny, rod, sausage, fuckpole, joystick, tallywacker.

Did he want me to name my vag?

There are so many options, here is a list of names for the female genitalia:

- Fanny, noon, pussy, flower, vertical smile, taco, meat curtains, muff, poonani, minge, pootang, axe wound, gash, foo foo, snatch, coochie, wizard sleeve, hoo ha, penis fly trap, hairy potter, Lawrence of a labia.

I do recall a time when a guy said he loved 'fucking my clunge'. Well, that killed the moment.

A toilet plunger was the first thing that came to my mind when I heard that word. Ramming it in and pulling out continuously until you're satisfied with the end result.

Now back to Junior, who did not perform at his best. He was quick, paid no attention to my vagina and rolled over straight afterwards to get ready for bed – what a let-down. I went to the bathroom, and that's when I noticed a jug of water next to the toilet. I shouted out to him and asked what it was for. It turned out he dipped his penis in it. He explained it's for hygiene reasons. He probably dipped his penis in that jug for longer than he did in my vagina.

The next morning, his alarm went off at 5 a.m. He said he had to be at work at 7 a.m. but had to be at the gym for 5.30 a.m. to work out. *Wait! You're telling me to leave your home at 5 a.m.?* It was pitch-black outside. He had a naked woman lying next to him – how about having cardio fun with her?

Can sex be classed as exercise?

Berkely Wellness states, "Having sex certainly counts as physical activity and sometimes even reaches the level of 'moderate' exercise. ... Sex does not burn as much energy as a non-horizontal workout for most people, either. The oft-cited statistic that 'sex burns 100 to 200 calories per session' is more overstatement than science."

This is when all my years of bad dates came flooding back to me. I confidently announced to his face, right there and then, that he was rude for chucking me out. Also, for someone in the line of work that he was in, he should have been ashamed that he couldn't make a girl orgasm.

Junior hadn't an utter clue. I walked out into the pitch-black feeling like Sasha bloody Fierce!

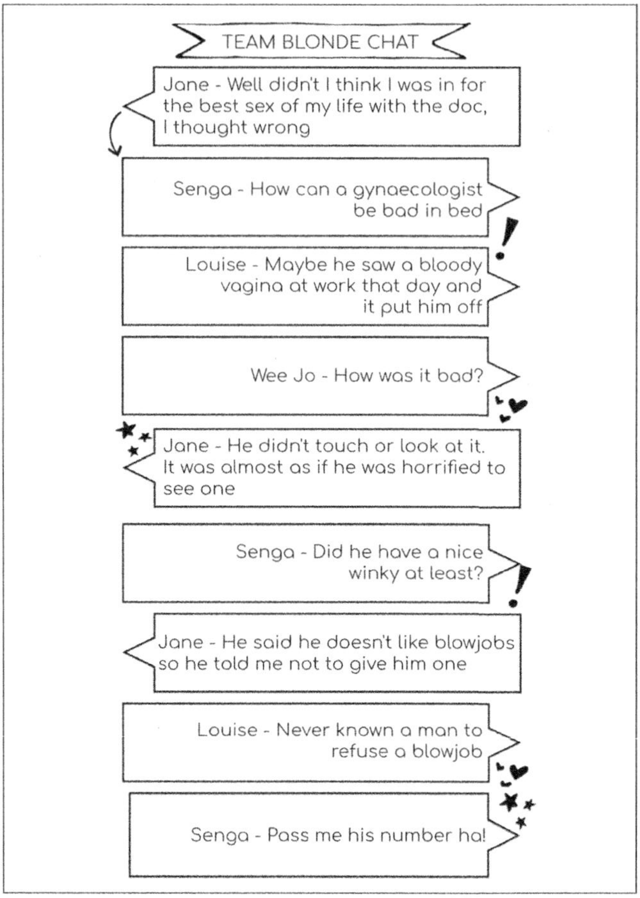

Tips

1. If the foreplay is not up to scratch, the sex could potentially be terrible.
2. If someone having kids (or not having kids, wanting them or not in future) is an issue for you then find out early on before you waste each other's time. Also try to find out if your date has an ex-wife/husband or anything else hugely relevant to you before you meet – whatever is a deal-breaker for you.

3. If he has a name for his penis, there may be some underlying issues there…especially when it's accompanied by a childlike voice – gave me the ick!

Socks, cocks, and broken vaginas

I was scrolling through the potentials on an online dating site when a notification came up: 'There are no other people in your area'. Great! I had run out of men. I extended the search radius but ended up matching with people in Belfast – that wasn't going to work.

What else could I do to find more matches? The only other option was to up the age. I was actually curious to see what the older men looked like. There I was swiping men who could potentially be the same age as my dad, and I ended up matching with a man called Spencer who was nineteen years older than me. He very quickly asked if he could call me, because he wasn't on the app regularly. I liked the maturity that showed – calling straight away rather than hiding behind a screen. We spoke on the phone, and he was charming, seemed to have his life together, and came across as very intelligent. I was gutted I hadn't increased the age sooner; this seemed like the way forward.

After a few calls, we agreed to meet. Both of us had busy schedules, and the only way a date could work was if it was at breakfast time. He was staying at a nearby hotel, so we agreed to meet there.

As soon as I met him, I knew, before he even opened his mouth, that he wasn't for me. He was wearing his jumper round his shoulders – *Did I just walk into a tennis club?* I will never understand that look. It's a jumper – you put it on. Put your arms through the sleeves, and voila, all complete. He might as well have saved himself some pennies and worn a scarf. Now, onto the footwear – he was wearing loafers without socks. I started to think about the amount of sweat his feet would produce throughout the day ... his loafers must have been stinking.

Spencer's breakfast was included with his room, so he said I could pay for mine at reception. Oh, okay, the gentleman I spoke to online was definitely absent. In my opinion, if you have been asked out on a first date, then I tend to think the person who did the inviting should offer to pay. I'm all for paying my way, it just seemed in this case it felt like he was perhaps testing me. He was sending me off to settle my tab the moment I arrived before any real conversation had started, it wasn't classy.

I always think drinks on a first date is a good option because it doesn't get as pricey as a meal, unless you decide to go for the champagne and shots – highly unlikely on a first date. If date two happens, I'm always more than happy to pay my share. This so-called gentleman earned a very decent pay packet, though it was by no means the reason why I decided to meet him – personality is always the key for me. I have met a few very wealthy men, and they always seem to be tight with money. I guess that's why they are wealthy – they never put their hands in their pockets.

Off I went to pay for my breakfast. By this point, I knew the date wasn't going to go any further. When I came back, he was curious to know when I had last been on a date. It had been the week before, but I thought it was best to say a few months ago to avoid too many questions. I asked him the same question. He mentioned his last date had been the month before, and she had ended up in hospital during the date.

'Hospital? What happened?'

'I broke her vagina.'

Let's just reiterate: HE BROKE HER VAGINA! I instantly felt my own vagina tense up.

He was so blasé about it, it was as if he didn't think I would be in shock with what he said. How had this charming older gent turned into a creep in less than five minutes? Now, let's discuss:

- Why would you bring this up, especially on a first date?
- Why do you think telling me this will make me want to go on date two, let alone let you anywhere near *my* vagina?
- How did you break it?

I stared at him for what felt like an eternity before I could ask him what happened. He explained that he was well-endowed down there, and she had a very tight flower. The woman in question had only slept with one other person. So, now I knew he had a big penis. Not only that, his third leg chat had made him a total wanker.

I had this visualisation of her vagina and it reminded me of the time I had to go to Sandyford sexual health clinic. I had noticed my vag was sore when I was peeing, oh no! Please don't say I have the clap. I spoke to the universe and declared I would use a condom for ever more if I got the all-clear.

I arrived at the clinic and as I walked in, I noticed all eyes were on me. Everyone staring wondering what I might have - is it warts, gonorrhoea, a rash, is she pregnant? I was doing the same look at each of them. Has he ripped his foreskin? Are they here for free condoms and lube? Is she wanting to discuss contraception?

I was as curious about what the other patients were in for as they were of me. In the waiting room, the majority of people are in the age of early twenties, there are some couples but mainly individuals with their head down and earphones in. My name is called out in the quiet waiting room, which is even more mortifying as it's not like you are at the doctors and you could have a sore knee, everyone knows it's to do with your vag. Will they be thinking I was a slag? I certainly felt like one at that precise moment. In I went and that's when I pretended I was a golden patient.

Nurse: I'm just going to ask you a few questions before I take a test. How many sexual partners have you had? Fuck! Should I whip out the names of all the men I have stored in my notes in my phone? It had started to grow at rapid speed. If it was ever found, I would have to pretend it was names I was considering if I was to ever have a baby boy. Should I ask the nurse if blowjobs are included as you can still catch a STI from a blowie. Should I pretend I'm in a relationship?

I significantly lied to her and said I've slept with four people and currently in a relationship. I wonder if she can tell I'm lying through my teeth. She continues to ask if I have any symptoms. I mention it stings when I pee.

She proceeds to ask if I have travelled abroad or slept with someone from another country. Absolutely! Backpacking without a shag with someone from another county is unheard of. I've ticked off six of the seven continents, still waiting for my Antarctic bonk. I say no as I don't even know the first names of the men, I only know them by their country. Big up to Uruguay and New Zealand.

She mentions I'm due my smear so would I like it now since I'm here which I opt for. Then the awkward moment happens, can you take off your underwear and place your feet in the stirrups. She told me to let her know when I'm ready. I had shaved to perfection but then I thought will the nurse think I've been lying about having a boyfriend if I'm clean-shaven? Should I have grown a big bush so she thinks I'm so comfortable with my imaginary boyfriend that I don't need to shave?

The nurse is now in front of me with her gloves on and some lube ready to put it on the spatula. She inserts it and her face is basically in my fud*. I think of how many different vaginas she sees in a day. Does she question how they look? How many have smelt bad? I also wonder if anyone has ever farted in her face.

Should I ask if she knows the gynaecologist I shagged who called his little man Junior? The nurse asks if I have any holidays booked with my boyfriend. My boyfriend? I don't have one, oh shit 'I do', I mention we're off to Italy (shut the fuck up Jane, stop with the web of lies). Turns out she's just back from Italy, of course she is, just my luck. The nurse then asks where I'm going in Italy. Before you know it I'm off to Venice, as it's in on our bucket list to go on the gondolas.

After the examination, the Nurse explains I have a urinary tract infection and I'm quite red inside. We chatted about what it could be, she asked if I've used any different washing powders or toiletries and it turned out to be the bath bombs I was using. There we go, I'm sensitive to bath bombs which I had been using every night which led to an infection. I was clap free, a round of applause for me.

Luckily now the STI checks are less embarrassing, you can swab yourself from behind the curtain. Insert a swab and circle around your vagina for one minute and results are back within two weeks (or two days apparently if you have a STI). The nurse said goodbye and said she hoped I had a lovely holiday with my boyfriend In Venice. I'm sure me and my 'fake boyfriend' will have a delightful time.

For all those interested: Spencer's lady-friend with the injury was fine, but I am sure her online bio will be saying, 'small penises only from now on'.

At this stage, I started to question why I bother. Where was I going wrong? I couldn't just blame online dating, because I had met just as many idiots in person as well. How did someone who acted like a gentleman on the phone and who had never mentioned anything with regards to sexual behaviour, think it was acceptable to blurt out a statement like that?

He asked to meet again. I said I had a busy month but I would be in touch, knowing I never wanted to see him again. I wish I could have said how I felt at that moment but I struggle to find the correct way to tell someone I think they are an absolute creep to their face. His online profile was so inaccurate.

Here's how it should have looked:

Bio: Older, well-endowed, tight-arse.

Interesting fact: I break women's vaginas.

Nicknames: Vagina breaker.

Dislikes: Socks and females who expect me to pay for their breakfast.

Likes: Jumpers as a decorative feature around my shoulders.

As I was leaving, he leaned in for a kiss, and I turned my face so he hit my cheek. I couldn't help but smirk. This guy was deluded if he expected me to engage in a kiss with him. That was the last I saw of the muff destroyer. The women reading this can relax their vaginas now.

TB Chat

Jane – Do you want a chuckle?
Senga – It's 11am, what could you have possibly done?
Jane – I had a breakfast date, within 10 minutes he told me he broke a woman's vagina
Weejo – What the actual FUCK?
Louise – OMFG
Senga – How does someone break a vag? How do you meet these weirdos?

Tips

1. I wish, there and then, I had told him it was unacceptable to talk about breaking a woman's vagina. Be upfront if a date says something you find unacceptable.
2. If a man talks about the size of his penis before you have even seen it, he is a first-class knob. Avoid! Alternatively, he perhaps has a micro-penis and is pretending he is huge.
3. To avoid wasting time, if you feel like a date won't go past date one, say 'It was lovely to meet, however, I don't think we are on the same page or have the right chemistry'.

Glossary
** Fud: Scottish slang word for your vagina*

I'm a killer in his eyes

Let me tell you about Christoff. We had been chatting for a while online. He had been away with work during our three weeks of getting to know each other. Once he returned, he arranged to meet me for a drink in a beer garden as we were having an unexpected summer heatwave. It sounded like an ideal first date.

While I was waiting outside the bar, I saw a man who was also waiting. I thought, *Is this Christoff?* I started to panic – had I got his picture mixed up with the other men I had been chatting to online? This can happen when you speak to a few people at the same time. The person anxiously waiting looked nothing like Christoff's picture. We kept looking at each other. I was doing that *Is-it-isn't-it?* look. I had it in my head that he was Christoff, and he was plucking up the courage to confess he had catfished* me. You hear about catfishing all the time.

I was just figuring out what my response was going to be when a girl went over to him, gave an awkward hug, and off they went. Saved by the bell! Poor guy must have been wondering if I was his date and also feeling confused.

Finally, my date arrived. He looked much better than his profile picture – he was stunning. So long to the person I almost accused of being a liar…now, that would have made an interesting story.

Off we went to the beer garden. It was idyllic and not too busy, so there were plenty of seats available. Christoff went to the bar for drinks and came back with my glass of wine and what looked like a gin and tonic. I asked him what type of gin he went for. He explained that his drink was actually lime and soda, he didn't drink; he was teetotal.

Teetotal? Why had he asked me to meet him at a beer garden? Why had he not mentioned it during our three weeks of chatting? Why hadn't he put this information on his profile? I don't drink a lot as to be quite honest, I'm a riot with alcohol. I'm a lightweight which means no shots allowed - bad things happen.

My friends and I often head to Sanctuary nightclub in Partick which is where most of my drinking fails have happened. I have fallen down the stairs in front of a guy I was attracted to. When I stood up, the only thing that popped into my head was 'Ta Dah!'

My friend Marissa matched online with one of the bouncers who was monitoring who entered the VIP section. Our aim was to get in there as let's be honest all the hotties settle in there. As she was wooing him I sneaked inside and was faced with dread. Two guys I had kissed and three I had slept with were all in this room, I was faced with five guys and not the tasty burger kind. Now this isn't a room you can hide in as it's fairly small, I had to duck and dive to avoid certain conquests. I came out to party and was left playing dodgeball for most of the evening.

It was in this club I experienced my first fight, I'm not streetwise in the slightest and managed to come out unscathed. I was hooking up with a guy who I referred to as Mr Pussy since licking out was his favourite thing to do. As we were queuing up to get our jackets, two girls behind us threw out a racial slur towards him, we had never seen these fuckwits before. He ignored them but I was not letting this slide. I turned to them and told them to apologise, they gave me abuse so I called one of them an ugly skank (best I could come up with since I was out my depth).

The said girl then launched for me and started pulling my hair. I grabbed her wrist to stop the pulling and I froze as if I was playing a game of musical statues. Marissa ran to get the bouncer who arrived immediately and chucked them out. As you can see teetotal me is probably for the best. Back to Christoff, I did find it odd how he hadn't mentioned being a non-drinker, which made me wonder what else he was hiding … Well, let me tell you!

Christoff came from Austria and his English was impeccable. He had an American-sounding accent and was very dreamy to look at. He explained he hadn't wanted to tell me he was teetotal in case it had put me off. It wouldn't have put *me* off, but it certainly could put many other people off, it's wasting other people's time.

He explained during the date that he enjoyed dating. He didn't have many friends, so dating let him get out and mingle with people other than his flatmate. I asked how many friends he would say he had. Two was his reply. Two friends? He had been living in the UK for five years and had only formed friendships with his flatmate and a girl he had met on a dating site. Why didn't he have any mates?

I started to question him. When I asked him what his hobbies were, he said he loved running. I suggested joining a running group, because it was a great way to meet people. He replied that he hated doing activities involving groups of people. Okay, moving on. What about his work colleagues? He said his workmates were all lads, and they only talked about cars and football, neither of which he was into. He was a hard nut to crack!

I gave up. I wasn't going to waste my energy on trying to find him pals, when he was clearly in no rush to make new friends.

The food menu grabbed my attention instead and I suggested we got something to eat. He stared at the menu for a while before pointing out that there was only one vegan option. Then he asked if we could head to a nearby vegan restaurant. *Vegan?* Oh no! Vegan *and* teetotal? I couldn't handle both. Was this the moment to tell him my favourite meal was a steak washed down with a glass of red wine?

Being the pushover that I am, I agreed to go to the vegan restaurant. I couldn't even pretend to be having fun anymore. I didn't want to be on the date, and nothing looked appetising to me. I decided that, on my way home, I was going to stop at a Chinese takeaway and get the full works – spare ribs, beef satay, a side of chicken balls. I could feel the saliva forming in my mouth.

The more he talked about the negatives of meat, the more I wanted it. His conversation during dinner consisted of how meat is causing cancer, the harmful effects of dairy, and why being vegan will help the environment. I have friends who are vegan but they don't rub it in your face. I signed up to a date, not a lecture on veganism.

This information was all far too heavy and serious for a first date. I wasn't going to waste my night any longer. Plus, the thought of the Chinese takeaway was getting me excited. It was the first time I've actually said face-to-face to a date that I didn't think we were suited.

I told him he was a lovely person, but I loved getting pissed with my mates and I *love* eating meat. Christoff would be best served by hanging out at vegan restaurants – the ideal location for him to meet like-minded friends or even, potentially, a date. The Chinese takeaway was incredible, in case you were wondering.

Side note: ironically I am now following a plant-based diet, maybe Christoff was my perfect match, bad timing I guess.

TB Chat

Jane – Last night's date was teetotal and vegan – both, not one, both!
Weejo – I could cope with someone who's vegan but not teetotal
Senga – Never trust someone who doesn't drink
Louise – I couldn't cope with that. How did you end it?
Jane – I was honest and said I like steak and red wine. That's enough for him to never want to message me again, I'm a killer in his eyes

Tips

1. In the initial chat about meeting up, ask your date what their favourite food/drink is. That way you can get a feel for if they are vegan/vegetarian or teetotal.
2. If a date has very few mates, you have to question why.
3. Do not be worried about telling your date that you don't think you are well matched. It was refreshing to get that off my chest. I wouldn't have been his ideal match either since at that time I ate meat.

Glossary

** Catfished: when someone fakes who they are. They tend to look completely different from their picture.*

Pus in boobs

Now I don't know about you, but sometimes, all I want is a no-strings hook-up. If you are not dating or in a relationship and do not have the advantage of a friend with benefits, then I am not ashamed to say a one night stand is the way to go. My mission to find a 'fuck buddy' was next on the agenda.

I got chatting to Shayne online. He was from the UK but now lived in France. He came over to the UK frequently for business and said next time he was over we should 'hang out', which translates as: have wild passionate sex in his fancy hotel room.

Shayne finally had a date when he would next be travelling to Scotland and our plan went into action. We met up for a spot of dinner at a restaurant I had always wanted to go to, and I was excited to start teasing and flirting – it's fun to flirt because it makes the evening more intense.

Shayne was cute. The first things I noticed were the smell of his aftershave and his tailored suit and how incredible his body looked in it.

A slight issue though, he was wearing walking boots with his suit trousers, he clocked me looking and replied that he had to break in his new boots as he had planned to go for a hike whilst in Scotland. I have no words.

During dinner, Shayne was acting slightly odd. He came across differently to how he was online. We had spoken on the phone a few times, and he had been pleasant and funny. Yet face to face, he was like a completely different person. He enjoyed telling me facts about anything brought to his attention.

Sushi was brought to our table, and he went into depth about the Japanese culture and history – to be fair, the geisha story was interesting, and he gave me the name of a book I should read on the subject.

Next, he ordered a bottle of red which originated in France. You guessed it, the history of France and facts about the wine were the next topic of conversation. My brain was expanding with all this new information. It was fascinating hearing his stories, but the delivery was very matter of fact. I was sure he could win a quiz show with all that knowledge. Also a bit odd – he didn't laugh when I said something funny. He just looked at me as if he was processing it. He put his hand out on the table and told me to look at his finger. Holy fuck! His finger was the size of a sausage. It was not what I wanted to see while chewing on my sushi.

He told me he was allergic to plasters and had accidentally kept the plaster on longer than he should. Why would he show me his swollen fat finger? Now, all I could think was please don't put that anywhere near my vagina. His finger made me feel sick. It was red, throbbing and leaking a bit of pus. Imagine if he slipped it in, and I assumed it was his penis, because let me tell you that finger had some girth to it. It looked like ET trying to phone home. Would my vagina get infected? Would it be rude to ask him to wear gloves or Marigolds when we got intimate?

At the start of the date, my horny level had been high. Now, it had dropped to around fifty percent thanks to finger-gate. I needed to get that percentage back up again as I had not had sex in months and was afraid my vagina was going to develop cobwebs.

Unfortunately, the horny level went down again when he told me about his two pets. When I hear the word pets, I tend to think of cats and dogs. Shayne had two cockatoos. He showed me images of his beloved 'kids' as he called them. He told me he let the cockatoos fly anywhere in his flat. I was picturing bird droppings all over the surfaces.

Horny level hit zero. Shayne liked to put his 'kids' in a backpack and take them around the local park so they could see the outside world. I could imagine the stares he'd get.

'Mummy, mummy, why has that scary man got birds in his rucksack?'

'Don't stare kids, he must not be well.'

I guessed locals had nicknames for him like 'birdman' or 'coo-coo man'.

We left the restaurant and headed to his hotel room. I was quite tipsy and started to brush off what I heard so far. As soon as I entered his room he announced that he had to iron his clothes for his meeting in the morning and said he wanted to do it immediately so he was organised – talk about a passion-killer. There I was, sitting on his bed, waiting for him to iron his shirt, trousers, jacket and tie … I didn't know ties even needed ironing.

I had well and truly sobered up after watching him iron and told him I wasn't feeling too good. He walked over towards me and began to kiss me, and it turned out he was a great kisser. I still wasn't turned on though. All the weird things that had happened came back into my head and it had put me off. He started to caress my breasts. Okay, good – he knew what he was doing. Should I give him a sympathy shag?

The horny level started to creep upwards. He stopped and looked at my nipples then proceeded to tell me my nipples were two centimetres away from the outer edge of my areola. If he was willing to stop to tell me about the size of my nipples, I certainly wasn't letting Sheldon Cooper* near my vagina.

Okay, that was it. I couldn't do this. I told him I had changed my mind, and he was too intense for me. I didn't want any more inspections, I now wondered if my areola was 'normal'.

Breasts obviously come in all shapes and sizes. Bra sizes can range from AAA cups to believe or not size N. The average sizes range from B-D cups. I grabbed my belongings, told him I best be heading home. He wanted me to stay but I feared he would measure my other nipple. What happens if it was more centimetres, not worth the anxiety.

It was time for the walk of shame, I mean the stride of pride.

On the plus side, the book he recommended was actually fantastic. You have to take the positive from any situation!

Tips

1. If you have any infected body parts, do not show a date – it's off-putting.
2. If you need to iron or do any household chores, do it before you meet the date or in the morning – it's a passion-killer and slightly rude.
3. Do not get all factual on a date – it's a date, not a lecture.

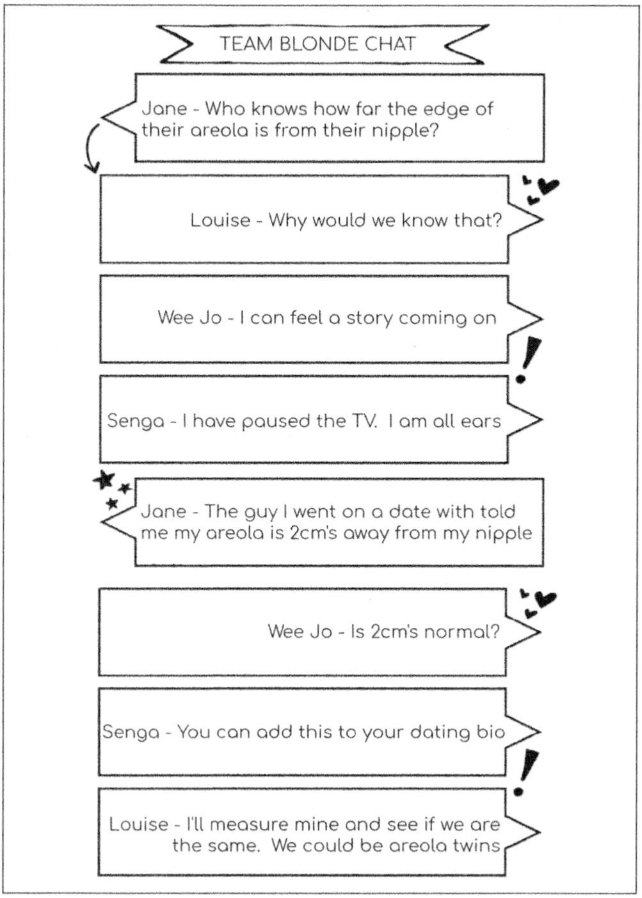

Glossary

** Sheldon Cooper: A fictional, genius-level IQ character with a lack of social skills in the US series The Big Bang Theory*

Early birdie special

I was working at a golf event one summer, which involved staying away from home. I thought it would be a good opportunity to fire up the online dating since I had been absent from it for a while. On the first day, I set the location parameters to within one mile on the app, so I would only match with attendees of the event.

I matched with a man called Edward who was working as a camera operator. Our schedules never matched. Whenever he was free, I wasn't and vice versa. Arranging a meet-up was tricky. After speaking for a few days, we were both desperate to meet. He asked if he could take me out for dinner, but I insisted we meet briefly at the event before committing to dinner because I wanted to be sure I would enjoy his company. His pictures online looked good, and he was outdoorsy which was a plus for me. I am into adrenaline sports, so it was nice to chat about that with someone with similar interests.

Now, I had three pairs of shoes with me at this event. Four-inch heels for walking clients to their suites (aka my ugly shoes), my uncomfortable six-inch stilettos (which elongated my legs) or when I saw a handsome chap, and a pair of flat shoes for when my feet could no longer handle the pain of being in heels all day.

One time, I spotted a gorgeous-looking man coming towards the suites, so I flicked off the ugly heels and replaced them with the killer heels. While I was walking the client and giving him my best chat, my heel got stuck in the carpet, and I couldn't move. I was genuinely that girl who had to take her foot out of her shoe and retrieve it from the carpet where it left a hole. Red face and dignity lost in the space of thirty seconds.

Ten minutes before Edward was due to arrive, I tottered off to the patio in my stiletto heels. I was a tad nervous. He had a great job, was good-looking, well-travelled... so with a few encouraging words from my colleagues and a touch-up of my makeup, I was ready for the meet and greet.

Coming towards me was an older man in his sixties. He had long grey hair and was holding a camera. That was definitely not him. He must have sent a friend to say he'd been called last-minute to shoot something. The man I had matched with was in his forties.

The old man said, "Hey, lovely, it's great to finally meet you".

Our security guy for the suite actually laughed out loud. I had just shown him a picture of my expected date, so he now knew that I'd been catfished.

I said, "You look completely different from your pictures".

He replied, "I'm just older now; I never take pictures of myself".

How rude! I couldn't believe this fraudulent man was casually admitting he'd used old pictures.

"How old *are* your pictures?"

"No idea. Some are from my travels ten years ago. I hope that hasn't put you off."

Ten years ago? That man had not aged well. He had short hair in his images. Looking back on it now, some of his images were in black and white which can be very deceiving.

When I asked him why he had lied about his age on the app, he said it was the only way he could match with younger women. If I was after a sugar daddy*, I would have set my max age limit on the app to sixty.

I made my excuses and said I had to attend to some guests. I didn't even let him say goodbye. I immediately blocked him on the app knowing he would take the hint from that.

I can't believe he thought he could get away with using old images. One of the pitfalls of online dating is that pictures can be deceiving – images can be filtered, taken at good angles or not be current. I was grateful I met him for those quick five minutes before arranging to go out for dinner. If I'd arranged to meet him for the first time at dinner, I would have been furious that I'd spent time on my hair and makeup to impress a man who could have been my grandad. Beware, everyone – catfishing is still rife!

One of the things I have noticed from working at events is the amount of married men who flirt with you or offer to take you for dinner. Some men are bold and keep their wedding ring on. They give you a look that says, 'I just want some fun while I'm away from home.' When you question their wedding ring, the excuses are:

1. 'I'm separating from my wife, I totally forgot about the ring.' The first thing people do when they separate is take the ring off. I'm sure the men saying this expect me to believe they are telling the truth – bless.
2. 'My wife and I have an open relationship.' Maybe you should tell your wife that?

3. 'Different postcodes have different rules.' Ah, so that makes it okay then.

Then there are the less bold ones who take their ring off but forget you can see the ring dent or tan line. It honestly makes me doubt the male species. What happened to vows? Is marriage a complete sham? It's in those instances, I question whether I want to get married.

Some Pros and Cons of Marriage:

Pros

- Sign of commitment.
- Financial and tax benefits.
- Apparently, you live longer if you're in a happy marriage.
- Religious belief.

Cons

- Getting married can cause extra tension in a relationship if the woman doesn't want to change her name on official documents.
- Marriage can extend the time couples in an unhealthy relationship will stay together - too many consequences if they split.
- Cost of wedding.
- Divorce is costly if you decide your marriage isn't working.

It's a lot to weigh up. I like the thought of getting married, purely so I can wear an expensive ring, go wedding dress shopping, receive lots of presents, and stay in the honeymoon suite.

Of course I'm kind of joking, it would be for reasons such as showing the final commitment. Sometimes, the fear sets in when I recall these arsehole men who cheat on their wives. Will I ever say, 'I do'? I'll leave it in the hands of fate.

TB Chat

Jane – I experienced my first catfish experience, I can now say 'I have been catfished'
Senga – Tick in the box
Weejo – What's catfished?
Louise – How different was he to his pic? Catfishing is when someone doesn't look like their picture
Jane – He was 10 years older, long grey hair, probably very saggy balls but I didn't chat long enough to find out
Senga – Well, that would be some story if you had seen his saggy balls.

Tips

1. Black and white images are misleading. If the chat is going well, ask your date to send you a picture that's not on their profile. You can make a joke of it or if they say they're off to an event, ask them to send a picture in their outfit.
2. Look up your date on social media to see if you can source other images. We all want our best pictures on our dating profile.
3. If you have been catfished then mention that they look nothing like their images. They need to be called out.

Glossary

** A sugar daddy is a wealthy older man who buys gifts for a younger woman in exchange for company or sexual favours.*

Would you like lies with that?

Kevin and I had those perfect dates. You know the kind of dates, the ones where you've been in a venue for hours, and you're shocked at how the time has flown by when the lights come up. On our first date, we went to a bar and neither of us drank because we were both driving early the next day. Chatting for five hours sober and still wanting to hear more from him was a good sign. We spoke about our hobbies, countries we had visited, and the different careers we had experienced. He was shy but came out of his shell by the end of the night.

We went on a few other dates, chatted regularly, and it was the first time in a while I thought this could potentially lead somewhere. He was intelligent, sporty, and his shyness was endearing.

He had called me at the weekend and invited me to his place the next day. Yes! It was going to be the night I got to hook up with this charmer. Many things go through my head when it comes to 'The Night'. Do I need to shave, wax, fake tan? What scent of body lotion should I use? What perfume? Then the clothes. What do I wear? I have two cupboards full of clothes, yet I still go on a mad panic-buying spree because I am convinced there is nothing suitable to wear. Then the underwear. Do I wear French knickers, a thong, cute pants, suspenders (hmm … maybe suspenders are too much for the first time he sees me naked)? Then my hair. Do I wear it down, plaits, a bun, curly?

As you can see, there are many decisions to make when it comes to the first night of intimacy. I wonder what guys think about before a first date? I asked a few of my males friends and was pleasantly surprised. Majority said the week before they would get a haircut if it's needed. One of my male friends said he avoids anything too heavy for dinner the night before so he's not bloated or farty (clearly Raymond didn't keep that in mind for our dates).

My friend Adam said he was flossing before his date was due to arrive and the floss got stuck in his tooth and he couldn't get it out. He was yanking away and his gums started to bleed, his date was literally arriving in two minutes time and he said he has never felt so anxious and hopeless. He said he went into the restaurant with the now blood-soaked string hanging out his mouth looking like a vampire and asked the waiter for scissors to cut off the excess string. Once cut off he was left with a tiny piece stuck in his tooth.

His date arrived and he said she must have thought he was odd as he kept trying to use his tongue to push it out. He didn't hear from her after the date, hence it was a date fail due to floss. What a shame when all he was trying to do was have a clean mouth. My friend Max swears by having a wank before a date so he isn't too horny and also won't cum too early if there is sex on the table.

Back to Kevin, Sunday morning came, and I woke up so excited. This guy was honestly perfect. I had fake-tanned the night before and was ready to show off my pins. Unfortunately, Kevin messaged me on Sunday afternoon with some bad news – he was in hospital. He had been playing basketball and had torn his ligament. Instantly, I wanted to go see him. He said his parents were with him and couldn't stop apologising for ruining our plans. Of course, I wasn't annoyed; I was more upset for him.

When he was discharged from hospital, he had to move in with his parents because there wasn't a lift in his apartment block, and he couldn't walk. For four weeks, we spoke every day but without meeting up as he couldn't drive. I had only just begun seeing him, I didn't want to meet his parents yet. I offered to pick him up, so we could drive somewhere, but he said he would rather wait until he was fully mended.

When he was finally back on his feet four weeks later, we arranged to meet the next day. I was so excited; it had felt like the longest wait. My friend and I went out the night before I was due to meet Kevin. We decided to explore the new area I had moved to.

Now, this is why I believe in fate. My friend and I had no idea where to go, so I randomly stopped two guys as they were walking out of a bar to ask if it was busy, any good, etc. One of the guys asked where I was from seeing as I didn't know the area. When I mentioned my hometown, he said he actually lived close by and explained where he was from.

'Clydebank? That's so funny, the person I've been dating is from there.'

The guys asked how old my date was and what his name was. Then there was silence.

'How weird, we know him.'

One of the guys asked, 'So, you're actually seeing Kevin?'

'Yeah, that's right, but I've not seen him for a while as he tore his ligaments, but I'm staying at his house tomorrow.'

The guy said, 'I'm sorry to be the bearer of bad news, but he went on a date with my girlfriend's best mate last week. His mum dropped him off, and he was on crutches.'

I instantly felt sick. I was devastated. He had been the one calling me every day, because he was bored as he couldn't get around anywhere. He was the one who didn't want to meet until he was back on his feet, and he was the one asking me to stay over at his house.

My night was ruined. I couldn't enjoy myself after that news.

I didn't want to call him straightaway, because to be honest, I thought I would start crying.

The next day I woke up to a message from him saying he was looking forward to seeing me. I called him and I told him what I had heard. Ironically, he didn't have a leg to stand on. He had no choice but to admit it.

He said he had been dating a few people, as he wasn't sure who he liked best yet. Now, I totally get that people multi-date, but after four dates then four weeks of speaking every day, surely, he should have decided by now who he did and didn't want to continue seeing. How long does it take you to decide if a girl or guy has the potential?

As a rough rule, two months should be a safe amount of time to broach the subject. Nevertheless, every relationship is different, so if it feels right earlier, go for it. If it doesn't feel right at that stage, there are a few steps you can take to build yourself up for the conversation. Ultimately, it is very subjective.

The fact that he made the effort to see that other girl and not me was enough for me to not want to see him again.

TB Chat

Jane – I've basically been cheated on
Louise – Is this the guy you've been chatting to but not seen the whole time as he's injured?
Jane – Yes! He's been going on dates with another girl whilst injured
Weejo – Offt! That sucks, sorry Jane
Senga – Go find him and injure his legs again
Jane – All those weeks chatting for nothing, he was supposed to be a nice boy
Senga – Hate to burst your bubble but I don't think nice guys exist
Jane – Disney says they do, that's good enough for me

Tips

1. If your date admits to dating other people, they are clearly not ready for you to be their partner
2. If you find out information about them that you do not like, be honest with the person and explain what you've heard. Every story has two sides, so don't judge until you get the full facts.
3. Be careful when flossing before a date, maybe stick to dental sticks.

Eat, sleep, cheat, and repeat

A woman's intuition is a powerful thing. Us women can sense when something isn't right, and not only that, we are fantastic at getting to the source of the truth.

Research on non-verbal communication skills has clearly shown that women are, as a group, better at reading facial expressions than men are. As a result, women are more likely to notice the subtle emotional messages being sent by others. If I have learned anything from my disaster dates, then it has to be: always go with my gut instinct.

I had been dating Sean for six months. It wasn't a perfect relationship, but I persevered because I know relationships take work. The reason why it wasn't perfect was that he didn't have a romantic bone in his body. What he did have was humour, and they do say laughter can be the way to the heart.

I had met Sean when I was working as a TV researcher. I had been sent to interview him about the Commonwealth Games being held in Glasgow in 2014 – he was a basketball player.

Now, Sean was 6 ft. 4", good-looking, and hilarious. He was childish throughout the relationship, sometimes I felt like I was dealing with a toddler. Nonetheless, you forget those moments when there are enough good times in a relationship.

One thing about Sean was that he never had money. He always said he spent a fortune on his sport, and he was a student, so that didn't leave much for himself. Our dates consisted of visiting each other – mostly me driving to him – and not actually going out.

I decided to take him out of his familiar surroundings and book a hotel; I wanted him to relax because he'd been training more than usual. As I had booked the hotel, he said he would treat us to dinner (that would be a first). When we arrived at the hotel, he said he didn't want to go out for dinner and would prefer a takeaway, so he could spend more time in the hotel with me.

It turned out that was a lie, the reason was he hated eating in public. Even though the dishes get washed, he didn't like the thought of other people he didn't know having eaten off a plate he was being served.

He told me to relax in the bath, and he would come back with a takeaway. Now, I am thinking Italian, Thai, Chinese…nope, he came back with a McDonald's. The reason why he chose this cuisine was that it didn't involve using plates from the hotel kitchen. The romantic night I had planned turned unromantic the moment I found out we were dining in with a McDonald's. I paid £150 for the hotel, and he spent £15. You may think £15 is steep for McDonald's, but he got a large meal, sides, and McFlurry for himself, while I got a medium-sized meal.

I had hoped, once his competition was over, he would be more romantic. One could always hope. Sean was adamant that we shouldn't be Facebook friends because his last girlfriend was psycho and was always questioning his innocent statuses – that was a warning sign right there.

Why is it that the women get called psychos when it's the men who made those women lose control? Men start to act secretive, and that's when the female intuition kicks in. My friend, Louise, is incredible at sussing out men. She honestly should be in the FBI. I just have to give her a name and five minutes later, she has images, related comments, blood and urine, family history, and shoe size – she is very impressive, my very own Sherlock Holmes. We aren't psychos, we are psychics.

Sean said he was still feeling anxious about letting any of his relationships into his private life. Okay, that's fine; I was curious to know what he was hiding but just brushed it aside. He said, out of interest, can I see your Facebook, so I let him take a look. He went through my pictures asking me to send some so he could keep them on his phone.

When he got to one picture of me and a girl I went to college with, he stalled. He asked if she was a friend. Lesley and I had studied together. I asked him if he knew her, but he said no, she just looked familiar. I instantly could tell he was lying. His body language had changed, and I was determined to find the underlying cause of it. I could tell he did know her; it was so obvious that he was lying.

The next morning, I messaged Lesley asking if she knew Sean, and she replied back saying he was dating her best friend, Ashley. Lesley continued on to ask how I knew him. I felt sick. My instinct had been right. I was so upset that he had been cheating on me. All those times he had said he was putting in extra hours at training had been a lie. He had been with her.

When I replied to Lesley telling her I was dating him, she instantly called and asked me for how long? Turned out he had been dating Ashley just as long as he had been dating me. The utter wanker. My friend put me in touch with Ashley. We were both in shock he had played us along for all that time. I had been nervous about speaking to Ashley, because I didn't want it to turn into a screaming match. We were both innocent and hadn't known about each other. Luckily, Ashley was lovely, and neither of us could understand why we hadn't left him sooner – we had both had the same doubts.

Of course, Sean denied it. He told me she was a psycho, then told her I was a psycho. Did the idiot not remember us telling him we were in touch with each other?

He even had the cheek to try to get us both back a few months down the line. I messaged her saying Sean was trying to get back with me, and she said he had sent her the same message. That boy had some nerve.

TB Chat

Jane – Sean is a PRICK! I swear this time, I AM DONE WITH MEN!
Louise – Caps are on, you must be livid. What happened?
Senga – About time you got rid of him, whatever it is will be a blessing in disguise
Weejo – At this point, can I say I've never liked him
Jane – He's been seeing me and another girl at the same time. How do guys like this get away with it for so long? I actually know the girl now – she's really nice
Louise – I bet he was making her pay for all his food as well
Senga – He's probably been living like a king with all that money spent on him by both of you
Weejo – Jane, please in future never buy things for a guy, unless you 100% trust him

Tips

1. If your date/partner doesn't want to add you on his social media be suspicious; they may be hiding something.
2. If you have found out a partner has cheated, block and delete their number, so you are not tempted to message them.
3. Listen to your intuition; I always felt something wasn't right.

Jane, at your cervix

I met Gordon at a sports event. He was fifteen years older than I was but was youthful and fun. I had known him for years, and we would see each other annually at an event I worked at. I referred to him as 'hot Gordon', and the girls I was working with adopted that name for him too. In great shape and always flirty, he was the eye candy we looked forward to seeing each day at the event.

Gordon walked into our suite one day with a bounce in his step. He admitted he was finally single and ready to start dating. I introduced him to online dating; it was honestly like Christmas for him. I helped him write his bio and uploaded his best images. He was eager to get started.

I watched him vigorously swipe left for his first one, then it was right, right, right, right …

Hold up, pal, your thumbs are going to fall off at this rate!

My male friends say a lot of the time they swipe right until they get a match, clearly looking for a quick shag then boys? I told him to keep me updated about girls he matched with. Each day he would show me his new matches, and he was delighted. He couldn't believe how easy it was to get a date. It was like he had a new lease of life – *Watch out, ladies, there's a new player in town.*

I told him I had matched with a guy that day, and he was taken aback that I was single. He asked me out on a date, but I said that he was too old for me.

"Nonsense," he said, "you're only as old as you feel."

He pointed out that he looked after himself and was a romantic. I told him I would think about it. Sure, he was good-looking and had a great personality and his peachy bum looked amazing when he walked past me each day. The thing is, if it all went tits up, I would have to see him the next year at the event, and I didn't want it to be awkward. I was also very aware that there's little point going on a date with someone who is recently single unless you yourself are just looking for some fun. I was looking for a relationship, so going on a date with Gordon would be pointless.

After the event was over, he messaged to say he was serious about meeting up. He encouraged me to go for dinner and said if I decided I was not attracted to him, then he would completely understand. I decided to go for it; it wasn't as if I was having much luck with the men my own age. We went for dinner the following week and I had a pleasant time; he was a gentleman and a fascinating businessman. From there, we went on a few more dates. I really enjoyed his company, though we purely met up for dinner and drinks. The only thing that was a turn-off was he kept mentioning recent dates and explaining what the sex was like.

I never understand why sex with other people should be brought up on a date. What do you want? A round of applause that you are regularly ejaculating? He mentioned the sex with his last date had been vanilla. Now, what does vanilla actually mean? According to Gordon vanilla was plain, boring, not adventurous, not memorable and, above all, not worthy of another try. If I decided I wanted to have sex with Gordon, it was clear I would have to give an Oscar-worthy performance like Halle Berry in the film Monster's Ball.

He went on to tell me about the different types of vaginas he had had the pleasure and not so much pleasure of. It was very educational. He categorised them as: saggy, old, designer, beef curtains, puffy, fatty and bony. He asked what I was – well, isn't that romantic? It was apparent he wanted sex, so fuck it, I'd use him for sex as well since he was not on my radar for a relationship.

He can now add me to his list of vaginas as the 'injured vag'. As when we were getting down and dirty, he flipped me over, so I was on top, and I felt a sharp pain. I suddenly got cramp and wanted to throw up. Off he went to get me water, and as I stood up to head to the bathroom, I realised I couldn't stand. The only way for the pain to disappear was to curl up in a ball on the floor. After googling my symptoms It turned out his big boy had hit my cervix – I didn't even know that was a thing.

After some rest and strong painkillers, I headed home on the train. It felt like the longest train ride. I was annoyed he didn't offer to drive me home after he witnessed the pain I was in. I realised he wasn't compassionate and only wanted his hole.

The thing about sex is so many things can go wrong. For women, the dreaded fanny fart comes to mind. Fanny farting, also known as queefing, is when air is trapped in the vagina, it is by no means flatulence even though it sounds like you're letting rip.

We've all been there; you're in the heat of the moment, it's passionate, wild, and romantic and it's suddenly all taken away by the sound of breaking wind or a squelching sound. Picture putting your foot in a wet welly and the sound it makes. Noooooo not now, why now when it's all going well. Will he be put off? Will he know it's not a proper fart? Will he tell his friends and they will all have a chuckle, it's mortifying?

Sometimes there is so much air that the noise will continue, it's making up a melody, the only way to stop it is to let it all out … take note from Elsa from Frozen and let it go, let it go, as you certainly can't hold it back anymore.

Air evaporates as well as your dignity. You pretend you don't care but inside you are dying.

The most common reasons why air gets trapped in your vag is down to sex and the position you are in. When you're sexually aroused your vagina expands which can allow air to enter. As the penis enters your vagina, it can push air further up which means there is only one way for the air to escape. Like Shrek says, it's better out than in.

If you feel you're about to let air out start moaning really loudly like Meg Ryan in *When Harry met Sally*, to cover the sound or perhaps play music during sex to drown out the foghorn.

After I got home that evening, I was just figuring out how to tell Gordon I didn't want to go on any more dates with him – the cervix stabbing wasn't for me – when a friend request popped up on my social media from him. I accepted it. About thirty minutes later, he messaged (not even to ask how my vagina was) to say he had been looking at my pictures and really loved one in particular. He screenshotted it, and I was completely taken aback. This image was from four years ago – clearly, he had a thorough rummage through my page.

I asked him what he liked about it. He said, and I quote, 'I prefer the skinny version of you.'

HE DID NOT JUST SAY THAT!

I was a size 6 in that picture, a time when I was working out excessively and was far too skinny. I was now a size 10 and comfortable with my shape. How dare he say that? A comment like that can not only make someone feel insecure but could lead to an eating disorder.

What an *arsehole.*

I said, 'Do you think I'm fat?'

He replied, 'No, I would say you are voluptuous; it's just the other you would be typically more my type.'

Well, you can FUCK RIGHT OFF THEN.

I will not have someone thinking that commenting on a woman's figure in a negative way is acceptable.

He couldn't understand why I was so upset and angry. He told me I was overreacting and being too sensitive. I could have stooped to his level and called him a wrinkly, decrepit old man, but I kept my dignity. Instead, I completely blocked him from my life.

That was the end of Gordon the fat-shamer and cervix jabber.

Tips

1. If a date mentions your weight, it's a reflection on their insecurity.
2. If a date has only recently broken up with someone; keep in mind they are probably just looking for a bit of fun.
3. If you feel pain on your cervix, take paracetamol, lie down and wait for the pain to disappear. After two hours I was back to normal, yes two hours curled up in a ball.

TEAM BLONDE CHAT

Jane - Gordon said he preferred the skinnier version of me. I'm actually really upset. He also fucked my cervix, I feel like I could handle childbirth now

Senga - Did he forget where the penis goes? Maybe he needs the birds and the bees chat again?

Wee Jo - How can he even say that? You don't have so much as a roll of fat. I don't even know where the cervix is

Louise - OMFG! He's old as fuck. He should be bloody grateful he has you. Get him dumped

Jane - Already done! Next?

Don't take the piss - part two

Surely, it couldn't get any worse than being pissed on? Hold my beer!

The majority of my pals have been cheated on. I have been cheated on a few times myself. I get that niggling feeling inside, and I know all is not what it seems.

Remember Alan? I had got back together with him after the urine incident, and no the reason wasn't that I missed the feeling of stale smelly warm water. I'll be honest though, every time he had to pee I got flashbacks and I never took a bath at his again.

The truth is I'm sure many of us have got back together with someone we know deep down that we shouldn't be with. Friends will be the first to give their opinions but sometimes the voice inside us will say maybe he's changed this time. He invited me to a family party which I felt was a big step as I met most of his relatives and friends which was comforting. It's always a good sign, the relationship seemed to be on a good track. Although meeting family hasn't always been plain sailing for me.

I went on a few dates with a guy I met in Sanctuary nightclub; he was from Jordan. When I went back to his place one day, he called me into the kitchen where I was faced with his family on Skype, waving at me and blowing kisses. He introduced me as his girlfriend which I definitely wasn't (this was not the time or place to discuss this situation with him).

His mum asked me what colour my eyes were. When I said blue, she started sobbing. He turned to me and said, "Mamma loves you". After the Skype session, I told him that we were not official, and he started to cry. It was all too much, and I ended it there and then.

Back to Alan, one night, he was working nightshift, and I was staying at his. He kissed me as he left and said he would see me in the morning. A few hours later, I woke up to my alarm. Where was my bloody phone? The sound was coming from under the bed. I must have knocked it off the bed when I was sleeping. I put my hand under the bed to grab it, and that was when I spotted another mobile.

Did he have a secret phone? Or was I being paranoid, and this was just a spare one? Why was it under the bed? Why was the picture on his screen a recent one? It was locked, so it wasn't as if I could look into it further. I put it back and decided I was overreacting and being silly. I decided that if I saw him with it, I could ask him then why he had two.

I was in the shower when he got back from work. When I got changed in his room, I noticed the mobile had gone. Okay, so now I *was* getting suspicious. The first thing he'd done when getting back was grab the phone. He had a night out with the boys that evening. I didn't want to argue as who knew what he would do if he was pissed off with me. He could flirt with other girls, if not more. I wanted to be that girl all his pals liked, the girlfriend who didn't complain, the girlfriend who the boys thought was perfect for him.

That afternoon, I dropped him off at his mate's house in the city centre, and he said he would come back to my place after the night out. He said it would probably be around one-ish as the boys were starting out early.

I was still awake later on that night so I gave him a call at 1 a.m. to see if he wanted to be picked up – it went straight to voicemail. I sent him a text – undelivered. I messaged his pal Brendon and said to let me know if they wanted picked up, as I couldn't get a hold of Alan. His friend wrote back saying he wasn't out with him that night. I instantly felt sick. Who was he out with? Why had he told me he was meeting Brendon?

I had a sleepless night; Alan didn't come home. My feelings were a mixture of worry, anger, and upset. The next morning, he called and said he'd left his phone in a taxi. I told him I knew he wasn't with Brendon. Alan had it all planned out. He said he was supposed to meet Brendon but randomly bumped into old school pals and decided to catch up with them. He was such an idiot.

I remembered our conversations where he had said he hadn't stayed in touch with anyone from school. In addition, why did Brendon have no idea they were supposed to have met? He blamed it on Brendon being daft* and said he must have forgotten. Alan couldn't even lie well.

The truth eventually came out when one of his friends told me what had really happened that night. Turned out, I dropped him off at the house belonging to a girl who he then hooked up with that night. There was me waving him off and telling him to enjoy his night, while he was thinking, *Oh, I will.*

I knew he had been with another woman. I couldn't deal with any betrayal. He ended it the next day, saying he felt I was checking up on him. Our first argument since getting back together, he gets caught out and *he* ends it – laughable.

During our relationship, he borrowed money off me. Who's been there before? You trust someone, they promise you they will give you the money back, yet you hear every excuse under the sun when you approach the subject matter.

I suggested, now that we had split up, he set up a direct debit. He made up an excuse that he couldn't get to his bank branch because it was miles away. I suggested he set it up online. His next excuse was that he didn't use online banking because he didn't trust it. As you can see, I was offering alternatives, but he didn't put any forward of his own. Eventually, he offered to drop cash off to me when he next got paid.

A few months later, after constantly asking for the money, he agreed to pop round with it. When he arrived at my flat, he mentioned his girlfriend was in the car as they had just been snowboarding, so he had to be quick. That suited me perfectly. I had no intention of having a chit-chat over tea and biscuits. He said he didn't have the full amount. Typical! I should have known it was too good to be true.

He then went on to say that if I wanted the money in his wallet, I would have to have sex with him. What a dickhead! Here are some reasons why I refused to have sex with him:

1. I had no respect from him due to the cheating.
2. His girlfriend was sitting in the car (he must have told her he was popping in to see a friend).
3. Why should I have to have sex to get money back that he owes me. It would be like a rubbish form of prostitution – instead of earning cash, I'd be reclaiming cash he owed me.

Let's just say that money was not handed over. I was so angry and even considered messaging his girlfriend to tell her, but to be honest, I just didn't want to open that can of worms. Instead, I pretended to him I was going to contact his girlfriend on social media and show her all the screenshots of the inappropriate messages he had been sending me.

That was enough for him to arrange to drop off the money later that week.

The day he was coming to mine, he messaged asking if my flatmate would be in. I thought it was odd. Why would that matter? I told him no, because I knew that was the answer he was looking for. My flatmate knew all about him and agreed to stay in his room and keep quiet. If I needed him, he would come save the day.

Alan arrived and, sure enough, wanted sex. I played along and told him I was still attracted to him and gutted he had a girlfriend now. I mentioned I was stressed, because I was worried I wouldn't get the money back. I started to flirt with him, telling him to give me the money and I'd reward him.

The money was handed over. He unzipped his jeans, and I shouted in my loudest voice, 'Steve, come help me.' The look on Alan's face was priceless. He shat himself. I mean, I think he might literally have shat himself. He left the flat immediately, and I *finally* had my money back. Lesson learned – be careful who you lend money to. What a dobber*!

You may question why on earth I got back with him, he is a bad boy after all. I think I really thought I could change him, maybe the time apart had made him see things differently.

From my experience now, I don't think people can be changed. If they have the bad boy persona then I think it will always be part of them in some way or another.

Why do girls stay with bad guys?

- We enjoy the excitement
- Bad boys have the confidence
- These type of men tend to be charming
- The usually ooze a strong persona
- They usually have more experience, thus know how to woo a woman
- Us ladies think we can change them

Above all, they fuck with your emotions. Absolute time wasters.

TB Chat

Jane – Alan demanded sex last night in exchange for the money he owes me
Louise – I would have recorded your conversation on the phone and sent it to his girlfriend
Weejo – Tell his girlfriend everything, he doesn't deserve a girlfriend
Senga – Did you have sex?
Jane – No chance, I pretended I was going to so I could get the money. Luckily, my flatmate was in to save the day
Louise – I'm so glad Steve was there. Alan is scum.

Tips

1. If there is a secret phone, be very suspicious. The phone is being used to hide something – that has to be questioned.
2. This is the tip I wish I had followed: confront your partner. I should have asked him why he had hidden his mobile. You need to hear their side of the story; after all, it could just be an old phone.

3. If you are owed money, suggest they set up a direct debit if they are going to struggle paying the full amount back in one go. Have evidence you have lent money, as that can come in useful if you need to take legal action.

Glossary

** Dobber: Scottish word to insult someone, 'You are a dobber'.*

** Daft: Scottish word for silly/idiot*

Grand old Duke of York

Patrick was an older gent (I'm starting to probably be typecast here), a man who was twenty-one years my senior. Now that I think about it, it was kind of odd – I would have been a baby when he was graduating from university. Patrick was a romancer; he could read women really well and was an incredible flirt.

I didn't see a potential relationship with him. He was going through a divorce and had three kids. It was very complicated, but I was happy to meet up, go on dates, and spend time with him. What I loved about our relationship was that we always had fun – no serious chats, no jealousy. We adored each other's company.

I turned up at his house one day, and he said, 'Turn around, I'm taking you somewhere.' He grabbed a backpack, took my hand, and we headed to the top of the Pentland Hills in Edinburgh. He laid out a blanket, got two glasses out of his bag and filled them up with Prosecco, complete with raspberries. Next, he laid out nibbles then played music through a speaker. We watched the sunset, it was very romantic and spontaneous.

At that moment, I thought, *I'm falling for him,* even though I really didn't want to. Patrick didn't want any more children and had plans for his retirement. I wanted children. It was never going to work.

One day, I went online to look through our messages to each other. I remembered he had mentioned a wine he loved, but he couldn't find it in this country. I wanted to see if I could locate it and surprise him with it.

I scrolled through the messages, found what I needed and thought I would have another look at the handsome pictures of him on his profile. It was then I noticed that his location was set as if he was abroad. I knew he was working in another country, but he had told me he deactivated his account after our second date.

He had actually got his phone out his pocket and showed me, not that I needed to see. Was that to make me believe I could trust him? Was it in the hope that I would delete mine, so I wouldn't find out something like this now? I hadn't deleted mine because I didn't want to lose our messages – he had said the loveliest things to me.

I decided to keep an eye on his profile. Maybe it was innocent? Maybe he was showing a colleague how to use it? Or maybe he was showing a colleague my profile? He returned to Edinburgh, and the day he landed, I went on his profile. Sure enough, the location said Edinburgh, which meant he had been online. I was gutted. Why was this always happening to me? Maybe it was a blessing though, as I needed a reason to stop dating him before I got too involved.

He got promoted the following week and told me he would be staying in London to celebrate with friends; he always sent me pics of the different countries he visited. I looked on his profile, and it said he was in York. Nooo! Now it was hurting. How was I going to admit to him that I knew where he was? I didn't want to ruin his weekend of celebrations. His messages were now getting few and far between. He sent me a pic saying, *Loving London.* I looked at the picture and saw an ice-cream shop in the background. Off I went to good old Google and typed in the name of the shop, and sure enough, that shop was in York. If you are going to lie, you need to do it well.

I wrote back saying, *Patrick why are you in York? My uni pals and I went to that lake/ice-cream place one day when we had time off uni.* I saw that he'd read the message, but he delayed getting back to me. Clearly, he was trying to find the best way to lie. He wrote back saying, *You're so good. Me and my buddy decided to take a road trip to York.* I wanted to say, *does your mate have a pair of tits and a vagina?*

On even closer inspection, I zoomed in on his sunglasses, and there was a woman in the reflection, sitting at a table, smiling at him. It could have been innocent, but I was doubtful. I swallowed my pride and told him I hoped he enjoyed the rest of his time in York. I didn't want to argue and would rather speak to him face-to-face. In my head I was really saying, *You cheating, old arsehole. You should be grateful I even entertained you ...* Ahhh, I felt better getting a hold of my real feelings.

Patrick always sent me pictures of him and his mates or work colleagues. It's not like I ever asked for any, it was just what he always did – maybe it was his way of reassuring me. He was away for four days with his so-called friends, and he didn't send me any more pictures.

The thing about us females is that we are damn good at finding information when we need to. I always say to my friend, Louise, that her investigation skills are being wasted. I don't know how many times she's helped one of the girls find something out or discover the truth with only a name.

When Patrick returned from his 'boys' trip, the excuses for why he couldn't meet me started. It was always: he was looking after his kids more often now, or he had friends visiting, or he had been offered more work. Something had changed, and I was ready to get to the bottom of it. I gave him opportunities to end it. I told him, if he wasn't feeling it, we should part ways, but he always said he wanted to be with me, it was just a difficult time. I was ready to walk away but I wanted him to admit the truth. The phrase 'have your cake and eat it' comes to mind.

It got to the point where three weeks had passed, and we hadn't seen each other. My gut instinct was to get out; I was feeling on edge and anxious.

I called him. There was no answer, so I left a voicemail, explaining that I felt he wasn't being honest, and it would be best to go our separate ways. He eventually called back, saying he was sorry, but he didn't feel ready for a relationship, which was where he felt we were heading. Now, why string me along all that time? Be honest.

I always like to think of the good that has come from a relationship. I guess I can tick off the list that I've now seen saggy balls. I mean not an obvious 'good' but let's say an experience.

TB Chat

Jane – I don't have the guts to tell Patrick that I know he was lying as he will think I'm psycho for stalking the pic
Louise – It's not psycho. He's the idiot for sending a pic which clearly wasn't London
Weejo – He's too old for you anyways, start finding a man your own age
Senga – Stick with him and get him to write you into his will!

Tips

1. If you have suspicions, get evidence first before you accuse.
2. If you think it won't go anywhere due to a date having too much baggage, then it's best to get out quick before feelings develop.
3. Think about the age difference – a twenty-one-year age gap is extreme. We both wanted different things because we were at different stages in our lives. In my case, I wanted kids and he didn't, so it would never have worked.

Fuckin' bronco

Danny and I had known each other for years from the local bars and clubs. He was very shy, and you would never see him chatting to girls, despite him being an absolute stunner.

I used to love it when I saw him on a night out; I knew he would be too embarrassed to come over and start a conversation when he noticed me entering the room. He would do the stare, aka eye-fucking, throughout the night, but it would be me who would have to toddle over and start the chat.

He played for the home football team and was regularly in the local paper for scoring and being man of the match. He never used to drink on nights out. I guessed he wanted to look after his body.

On a rare night when he *was* drinking, I found him very conversational, and he ended up asking me out on a date. *Finally* – that was a long two-year wait!

He booked us a table at his favourite Thai restaurant, Chaophraya. Well, at least I was getting the best of the best from him. I was nervous. He was shy. I wasn't sure if there would be a second date, because his shyness was too much. I led the conversation, but I almost felt like an interviewer. Not that I would normally condone drinking too much, but I wanted him to get drunk, so he could be conversational like that one time in the club. He was drinking his pint so slowly that he would never get drunk.

After the date, we didn't kiss. It was one of those awkward moments, you know, at the end of the date when you're trying to judge what the other person wants. Do you go in for a kiss, a hug, a wave …? I was getting nothing from him, so I opted for a hug. He went for a wave which led to his arm touching my boob. His face went red as I laughed.

I knew one of the boys in his football team and told him I had been on a date with Danny. I had said he was really shy, and the other boy said Danny had a micro-penis, so that was probably why. Oh shit! That could be it. Maybe that was why he was shy with girls – he was embarrassed about the size of his manhood. At least a micro is easy to suck. It's like a mini lollipop, the size of a tampon. For once, the blowjob doesn't feel like a job, as the penis doesn't even reach halfway in your mouth.

I felt sorry for him. He was a lovely guy. It must have been horrible getting slagged off by the other lads in the showers after a training session. The following weekend, I randomly bumped into him on a night out. He said he had really enjoyed our night and apologised for being shy, saying that he hadn't dated in a while. We arranged another date, but that night, we ended up back at his place. As we got out of the taxi I lost my balance, slipped and the world slowed.

I could do nothing but watch my face give the pavement my first kiss of the night. I face-planted onto the ground and scuffed my knees. Blood was trickling down my legs. I pretended it didn't hurt when he asked if I was okay as I didn't want to kill the vibe. It was actually painful, really I wanted to scream 'mother fucker it stings'! I had skin coming off my knees, but I put on a brave face and started kissing him to get the night started. What a kisser he was!

Who cared if he had a micro-penis? Maybe it wouldn't be so bad. As we were taking off each other's clothes, he excused himself to go to the toilet. He was in there for about fifteen minutes. What was he doing? Was he trying to stretch his penis? Was he using an Austin Powers penis enlarger? (I really want to watch that movie now, in fact, I wonder if I've ever met a spy who shagged me.) Was he taking pills to elongate his penis? Maybe he couldn't get it up? The fifteen minutes gave me time to clean up my knees and wipe off the dried blood. *These scars had better be worth it.*

When he came out of the toilet, I was greeted by his six-pack. The micro-penis thoughts were a distant memory while his abs were on display. The kissing continued, and that's when I felt a hard object against my thigh. How had he managed to get his penis so big? I mean, I had been kidding about the penis enlarger, but maybe it was a real thing? If that was the case, how long would it last for? I placed my hand on his penis, curious to feel the results of the penis enlarger. Well, well, well! It was massive.

Now, I was thinking he must have put on a fake penis. Poor guy, having to resort to that. He took his jeans off, and I thought, *that's one realistic looking penis.* It was then that I knew I had to tell him I knew about his condition … and I didn't want a fake phallus that size going anywhere near me.

I blurted out that I knew he had a small penis and that he didn't have to resort to using a fake one. He looked at me as if I was insane! He asked what made me think he had a small penis. I told him what his friend had said. He smiled and said, 'You've been wound up.' My face dropped, I wanted the ground to swallow me up. Why oh why, am I so gullible?

Luckily for me, he went in for the kill and I genuinely thought I was getting killed. I was imagining my eulogy would say 'death by a big, enormous cock which stabbed her internal organs'. My organs would probably be too damaged to even donate. Let me tell you, he would have given a horse a run for his money. The only saving grace was that I was still drunk so didn't feel the full extent of the pain until the morning, when he reminded me that I'd thought he had a tiny penis.

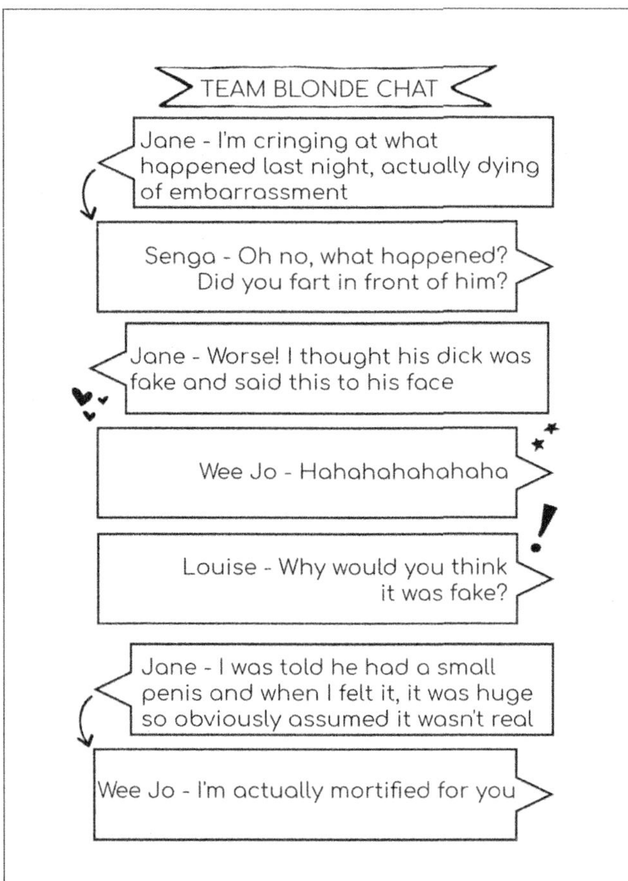

Mortified and red-faced, I left his apartment. My legs felt like jelly, I couldn't walk properly. A big willy is not for me, I was walking like John Wayne.

I still wonder what he had been doing in the bathroom for so long – I guess, if you've got to go, you've got to go, especially when it's a jobbie*.

Tips

1. Don't always listen to what others say about someone you're dating; you need to find things out for yourself.
2. Don't panic if someone is taking their time in the bathroom before getting intimate. They could be shaving, moisturising, freshening up, brushing and flossing their teeth, or maybe doing a poo and waiting for the smell to dissipate.
3. You shouldn't tell them a story you've heard about them. If I had just waited a few more seconds and looked down, I would have realised it wasn't fake and been saved the embarrassment. At least I gave him a story to tell next time he was at training.

Glossary

** Jobbie: Scottish word for a poo, pronounced 'jaw-bay'*

When the shit hits the scran

It's not always me who ends the dates. I have been stood up, not been contacted after a date, dumped by a guy so he could get back with an ex, cheated on, ghosted* after getting on well during a date and ... well, on this occasion, I don't blame the guy for not getting back in touch.

I had matched with Reece online, but I ended up deleting the app because I was going on a girls' holiday. When I returned a month later, I headed out to a bar with friends. I recognised a Ryan Gosling lookalike inside, and off I went to approach him. All that holiday sun must have given me extra confidence, because I wouldn't usually approach a guy I didn't know. The fear of rejection or the fear of the guy not being single would normally have stopped me.

Luckily, I had nothing to worry about as we hit it off instantly. I couldn't wait for my friends to see who I was chatting up. To my surprise, Reece mentioned that we had matched online, and I'd completely patched him. Oops, so I did! I had a lot of making up to do.

After one too many drinks and some cultured conversation – yes, I can be cultured – we swapped numbers, and we lived happily ever after. Ha! If only one of these chapters ended like that.

Reece and I met up for dates on a regular basis after that. Once, he even surprised me with flowers when he greeted me at his door – very romantic. It was almost like Ryan Gosling in *The Notebook*. See – true romance is not dead. He was studying for a master's in criminology; not only was he intelligent, he was also handsome, kind, and a great cook. He introduced me to his brother, who he was close to. It's lovely when you're introduced to the family – you feel appreciated and it lets you know that there could be a future in the relationship.

One night, we went to a seafood restaurant. I had my favourite dish, which is mussels, and he had a fish dish. It was so refreshing to be with him; it was easy, no dramas or stress. We had glass after glass of red, then headed back to his. I felt content and relaxed around him. As we walked into his home, we both started to feel sick. I was sweating and could feel the saliva gathering in my mouth. I ran to his en-suite toilet and threw up. Unfortunately for him, his came out the other end; he had chronic diarrhoea. I could hear the noise when his diarrhoea came out of him. I was too sick to even laugh.

There I was in one bathroom, constantly being sick, and he was in the other bathroom, gripping the toilet seat. All I can say is: Thank God he had two bathrooms, otherwise he would have been shitting on the floor. All dignity went out the window. He didn't come through to where I was, which meant his arse was still erupting. Oh, how grateful was I to just be throwing up. Thank God it wasn't the other way around. I wouldn't have known how to cope, not with him so close by.

Our romantic night turned into an utter nightmare. Hours went by. I couldn't understand why it wouldn't stop. I was literally hugging the toilet and going from hot to cold. I gathered up the energy to walk to the other toilet and knock on the door to ask how he was. I could smell the toilet before I could see it – a mixture of deodorant and shit. The smell was so bad it made me run back to my toilet to throw up again. He could have done with opening the window, but that was probably the last thing on his mind.

I shouted from the bedroom to ask how he was feeling. He said it was best to head home as he wasn't feeling any better. I didn't have the energy to move. No chance I could leave. i asked if there was any chance he could let me stay over and he opted to sleep on the couch. To be honest, that was definitely the best move – imagine waking up in the middle of the night covered in his shit?

This has happened to me before when I was around eleven years old. A second cousin I barely knew was coming over to mine for a sleepover. As we were getting into bed, she placed down a waterproof sheet; I was shy back then so didn't ask what it was for. I figured it may be because she pissed the bed. In the morning I woke up to a smell of poo and I had her faeces smeared onto my thigh. I ran to find my mum, who saved the day. She cleaned me up and it was never mentioned after that.

I, therefore, feel I've had my share of shit.

Back to Reece, I decided to leave water outside the bathroom door – poor boy would be severely dehydrated. As I was leaving the water outside, out came another squirt from his now stinking arse and I laughed aloud. He shouted, 'Go, please go.'

Shit happens!

Back in his bedroom, I put the TV on to drown out the noise. I eventually heard the bathroom door unlock, and he went straight to the living room. He didn't come through the full night. Drained and exhausted, I passed out.

In the morning, I woke to a text message. He said he'd had to go to his parents' for Sunday lunch and to post his key through the letterbox. I asked him how he felt, and he said fragile. I was slightly annoyed he hadn't woken me. Weird to just leave me – we'd both been unwell, not just him.

When I returned home, I messaged him, and received no reply. A few hours later, after calling him, there was still no answer.

Five years on, and I'm still waiting. Was it the embarrassment of the situation? Was it my laugh that sealed the deal?

Well, at least I got to experience dating a Ryan Gosling lookalike. When I see the actor on screen, I always think of the shitting incident – c'est la vie.

TB Chat

Jane – Reece had the shits after our date last night whilst I was chucking my guts up. Who said romance is dead?
Weejo – Thank God it wasn't you with the shits
Jane – He's not replying to my texts, do you think I've been patched?
Senga – He's maybe still on the toilet ha. I'm sure he will message
Louise – Bet he's mortified, I'm sure he will message when he's better

Tips

1. Don't opt for seafood in the early stages of dating. Out of all food, seafood has the highest risk of food poisoning.

2. Always pack a small bottle of perfume, mints and a tiny pack of wipes in your bag – a female survival kit.
3. If you feel like you're going to be sick or have the shits, LEAVE! Run as fast as you can from their place. I would rather have had an accident on the street like the scene from the movie *Bridesmaids* than at his place.

Glossary

** Ghosted: an expression used in dating when someone suddenly cuts all ties and communication with the person they have been seeing.*

Keep talking, I'm walking

I was doing a bar promotion that involved offering shots to any customers entering the bar. I saw a guy I thought was a bit of alright, went over with a drink and ended up speaking to him most of the night. As he was leaving, he asked for my number. I had been so caught up in online dating that it was refreshing to be asked out by someone in person.

We messaged for a week. I liked his honest attitude; he was opinionated, but that always boded well for good discussion. Scott met me in a bar for our first date. It soon became apparent that he would lead the conversation for the night. I can chat for Scotland, but I was struggling to get a word in. He would go off on a tangent, in the midst of deep conversations, never asking me my thoughts. I liked his confidence, but at this stage, he wouldn't have been able to tell me what my passions were or my profession was – yes, he saw me working in the bar, but I had been helping out a friend.

Then he started to talk about his achievements, how he could read women (could he read that I was bored and wanting to go home?), how women only used him for sex as word had got about that he had a large penis – his mates called him Trousersnake. Hadn't Justin Timberlake already snagged that title?

According to Trousersnake, the next reason why women fell for him was that he was wealthy. I honestly couldn't believe what was happening. He might as well have given me his bank statement as there were no secrets with this guy. He told me how much he earned, what car he had, what gadgets, and how many different businesses. He even said, 'What's not to love about me?' Wow, self-indulgent.

Once, when he was in Marbella with his pals, he booked a bed at a luxury beach resort and told me he was mingling with celebrities. *Oh lovely! What do you want me to say to that, Scott?* He said girls were asking him for selfies because they thought he must be a celeb, and he had loved every minute of it. Well, I certainly wouldn't be his type of girl. I would have begrudged paying the entry fee for the beach resort and would have ended up minesweeping* as I wouldn't be able to afford the drinks.

Scott managed to take a breather ... by breather, I mean: went outside for a cigarette. As you are aware, smoking is a no no for me. Even if Scott happened to be a 'nice guy', the smoking wouldn't have sat well with me.

He told me he had attended many events and sometimes hired an escort so he would have the best-looking woman in the room. I laughed, assuming he was joking. The stern look was enough evidence that it was no joke. What an actual weirdo. The guy who claimed that women fall for him all over the place had to hire a woman to go to an event.

I want to point out that this was one of the few things I said all night; I was surprised there was a gap long enough for me to speak my thoughts. By then, I had completely zoned out of the date. He excused himself to go to the toilet, and that was when I got a tap on the shoulder. It turned out to be a guy I used to work with. I was so relieved to be able to chat at last. Words coming out of my mouth felt so good! I felt like I hadn't spoken in an eternity.

Scott came back, and the first thing he said was, "I leave you for five minutes, and you're off with another man – typical woman".

Typical woman? It wasn't even a joke; he looked pissed off. I asked why he had that attitude when I was only talking to my friend.

"Do you flirt with all your pals?"

I said I was surprised he was letting me speak at all, since I'd not been able to get a word in all night. He called me a cheeky cow. Well, that was all I needed to hear. I grabbed my bag and left. He mentioned he had parked his Porsche on the same street as the bar and was going to collect it in the morning. He wasn't lying about the Porsche; I peered in the window and spotted a child's car seat. This was shocking on two counts: he hadn't mentioned having a kid and a Porsche is not a child-friendly car. If only there had been a newsagent open, so I could have got some eggs to crack over his car.

The only thing I learned that night from Scott was that some men hire escorts for events – I had no idea. I thought escorts were only for sex. It all adds up now though. I've been at events and seen stunning ladies with men who weren't blessed in the looks department or looked like they were nearing their deathbed. I will be sure to keep a lookout next time I'm at an event. I'll quiz the escort, I mean fake girlfriend, on his likes and dislikes. That should be a sure test. A psychologist would have a field day with Scott. He is egotistical, rude, over-confident, bragged about his wealth, and clearly doesn't let the person he is with speak.

TB Chat

Jane – I'm in the wrong profession, there are girls out there who get hired to escort men to events and they don't have to have sex. Drinks, dinner, and no random sex – where do I sign up?
Senga – If you find a link send me it ha
Louise – They must have sex, the guys will definitely be expecting it
Weejo – I agree, the guys will hope sex will happen after plying the girls with drinks
Jane – I'll try it and report back to you
Senga – Good lass!

Tips

1. If you come across a date who is rude, I would recommend leaving. If they show rudeness that early on then it's a red flag.
2. If you feel like you can't even enter the conversation due to their excessive chatting, it's a sign that this is a fundamental personality trait.
3. If you do spot a pal in the bar, and your date isn't going as well as you'd hoped, get your friend to help out by creating an emergency to get you out of the date.

Glossary

** Minesweeping: stealing people's unattended drinks or drinking leftover drinks.*

The Dominos effect

They say you meet someone when you least expect it.

I was waiting in a long taxi queue, scoffing a pizza, when I got chatting to Daniel. We bonded after he asked for a slice of my midnight feast, and I pointed out that I didn't share food because I was a greedy cow.

Daniel liked the fact I was holding my ground and said he would be shocked if I finished it – the challenge was on. I always like to keep a few slices to eat in the morning; I'm a fan of cold pizza. Reluctantly, I ate the full pizza and ended up looking six months pregnant – lovely.

Looking back, it's mortifying and how unattractive I must have looked trying to shove slice after slice into my mouth. Daniel high-fived me (very chuffed with myself), and we continued to chat in the busy queue. We laughed and people watched while we waited for the taxis to arrive. The taxi queue at 3 a.m. is always entertaining; you see couples arguing, people throwing up, girls crying, people singing at the tops of their voices, guys fighting…

It turned out Daniel was travelling in my direction, so we shared a taxi, and he paid – bonus – which was very courteous. Now I don't know about anyone else, but when I'm in a taxi after having way too much to drink, I tend to tell the taxi driver my life story. It's like being at the beauty salon, you end up telling the therapist too much information when you're getting waxed just to distract from the fact that they are looking at your overflowing pubes.

My friend once asked her driver to attend her wedding whilst she was off her face. Another pal begged the driver to set her up with his single son, she hadn't even seen a picture of him, desperate times and all that.

I vaguely remember telling Mr Taxi Driver I had impressed Daniel through my pizza efforts, and having a debate as to why pineapple shouldn't be a pizza topping (it really shouldn't in my opinion, fruit on a warm pizza makes me boak). Looking back it's so cringe. As I stumbled out of the taxi, Daniel asked for my number, and best of all, we decided to meet the next night for dinner. Maybe scoffing pizza in front of a cute guy was the way forward.

The next morning, I woke up to a message from Daniel – a very good sign. 'Good morning back to you, Daniel.' We messaged back and forth that day – also a good sign. I booked in a last-minute blow-dry, got my friend to do my makeup and spent the whole day beautifying for the date. Now I realise that might seem extreme, but bear in mind, he had witnessed me participating in the food guzzling challenge, slurring my words, and not looking my best the night before. I wanted to show him I could look glam.

Daniel was due to arrive outside mine at 7 p.m. I was shitting it (no seafood, I promise). My armpits were sweating loads, which resulted in me packing deodorant in case this kept happening throughout the night. He had said he would arrange the dinner reservation – I appreciated that. Also, I do love a surprise. I was hoping it wouldn't be a pizza place. I looked out my window waiting for Daniel's car to arrive. After fifteen minutes, I started to feel anxious.

I had last heard from him at 3 p.m. and all had seemed fine. Maybe he was running late? Maybe he was lost? My flatmate came into my room at 7.30 p.m. and said, 'Aren't you supposed to be being picked up at 7 p.m.?' I was too embarrassed to say Daniel hadn't turned up, so I said he'd changed the time and was picking me up at 8 p.m. instead. By this point, I was almost certain he wasn't coming to get me.

I called Daniel and it rang out. I could see that he was active online. As guys say, it was a real kick in the nuts. I messaged to ask if everything was okay – no reply. I could see the clock approaching 8 p.m. I didn't want my flatmate asking questions, so I got my bag and coat and left my flat. I was too mortified to tell him I'd been stood up.

My flatmate heard me leaving and shouted, "Let me know if you're not coming home so I can put the chain on the lock".

If only I could tell him the truth and not feel embarrassed about what had happened. I knew Daniel wasn't coming; it was soul-destroying not knowing why. He could at least have had the decency to not be active online, then I could pretend his phone had broken or he'd been robbed.

For two hours, I sat in my car crying. I'd spent money getting my hair blow-dried, done my makeup specially, and now my mascara was running down my face. Waterproof mascara is a makeup must from now on.

Maybe he'd got a flashback of me scoffing the pizza and realised how unattractive it was? Well, Daniel, at least I was up for a challenge and a laugh – they're good qualities to have. I had bigged-up Daniel to my pals, and I knew the messages would be coming in soon to ask how the date went. Should I tell them the truth? Or pretend I went on the date, but it didn't go well?

At one point, a passerby with his dog was looking at me from across the road as his dog was doing a shit. I thought nothing of it until I looked in the car mirror and saw mascara all down my face. Luckily, I always keep wet wipes in my glove box. I encourage you all to have them in your car, perfect for when you need to wipe away tear-stained makeup or if you need to pee in a bush if you're in the middle of nowhere, or for wiping under your pits if you are a bit stinky.

If he had changed his mind then at least he could have had the decency to message something, anything. Being ignored was the worst part. It is never okay to ignore anyone.

I went on a great date once, then never heard from the guy again. It was the oddest experience, because he had been the one to chase me. He kept saying throughout the date that I made him laugh, I was his ideal type, etc. Then I was completely ghosted. Ghosting can be a way of showing they don't want to take it further, but don't want to hurt your feelings so easier to block you. Basically, it's an easy way out.

Anyway, back to the Daniel dilemma. I went back home at 10 p.m. My flatmate was awake, and he said he hadn't expected me to be home so soon. I pretended the date wasn't good and laughed (I was actually crying, but it sounded like a hysterical laugh), shouting, 'On to the next'.

I was feeling low. I couldn't sleep and the thought of ever meeting a decent guy genuinely felt impossible. My radar seemed so off.

Being stood up is a horrible feeling. You question everything: am I not funny enough, am I not pretty enough, maybe he doesn't think I'm intelligent, or maybe he got a better offer from someone else?

Then you start questioning him: does he have a girlfriend or wife, has he been in an accident, did he lose his bottle?

If being stood up was like grief, I certainly went through all the stages. I will never know what happened to Daniel, but I do hope he had a bad case of the squirts that night and shat all over his fresh bedsheets.

TB Chat

Jane – I've been stood up! How can someone be so cruel?
Senga – Oh shit! What a bawbag! When was the last time you heard from him?
Weejo – Who does that to someone? What a heartless fuck! So sorry Jane.
Louise – I take it you've tried calling him?
Jane – I'M OVER MEN!

Tips

1. Ideally avoid spending money on getting a blow-dry/doing your makeup for a first date – save that for a special occasion. What a waste for me that day!
2. If you have been let down on a date, do not send an angry message to that person – you will not get the answers you want to hear. On to the next.
3. If you are stood up, don't pretend the date is going ahead; I sat crying in a car. What a waste of a night. Tell a friend – they will probably offer to buy you ice cream/pizza while you watch sad movies and cry.

Cheap impact

I was set up on a date through a friend who told me Marcus was a decent lad. It wasn't a blind date as I had met this guy briefly before at a party, though we had only chatted for a few moments, and he had a girlfriend at the time. Marcus lived in Edinburgh, and I lived two hours away.

He messaged me to say he had heard I was attracted to him – cringe! It worked though, and we arranged a date. I decided to travel to him as I hardly got to visit Edinburgh. He told me he would take me to Edinburgh Castle, then we would go for dinner and drinks. It sounded romantic.

On my way to the train station, I popped into Marks & Spencer's toilets, (an upgrade from the train toilet), to redo my makeup. When I put my bag on the floor, a continuous buzzing sound came from my bag. I heard a tut from the cubicle next to the sink I was using.

A woman shouted, "There's a time and a place to use that thing!"

Ha, brilliant! I located my electric toothbrush – sorry to disappoint – from my bag, switched it off and made a quick escape before having to come face-to-face with the woman. I didn't want to tell her it was just my toothbrush, because I thought it would make great gossip for her to tell her pals at one of their coffee mornings. Old ladies love gossip, the more shocking the better.

I arrived in Edinburgh, and as I got off the train, Marcus told me to meet him at the castle because he was running late. Great start. I began my ascent to the castle, and the wind was wild. My neatly straightened hair was a shambles.

He turned up twenty minutes late and apologised, mentioning his yoga class had run over. He laughed and said he had even skipped a shower to get to me quicker. Wow, no effort there then. He knew he had a date – couldn't he have skipped yoga for one night? Instead, he turned up with visible sweat marks under his armpits. Maybe the wind would help disguise the smell (after all, we all know I've had to endure worse foul smells). At least I didn't need to feel bothered about my monstrous hair, which had expanded in size due to the force of the wind.

We quickly made our way down to the main high street to get out of the gale. I asked him where he fancied going for dinner, and he said he'd totally forgotten about dinner and had already eaten. *Wow, selfish!* By that point, my belly was rumbling, and I was annoyed he had forgotten. Anyway, I didn't want to ruin the night. I was trying to stay calm and not make a fuss. We headed to his local bar, and as soon as we walked in, he told the barman to set up a tab. *Fantastic! Champagne, please?*

Throughout the night, we ordered three drinks each. I stuck to red wine, and he ordered three pints. I was starving but was still trying not to make a fuss. The only food behind the bar was peanuts or pork scratchings, and I wasn't a fan of either.

By luck, the barman put bowls of popcorn on each table – result! I was going to be raging* if Marcus dared eat any of the popcorn. After all, I was the one at death's door. Of course, the man who had had his dinner grabbed a large handful of popcorn and shoved it in his gob. I looked at him as if he'd just eaten my last Rolo. I desperately grabbed what was left and savoured the mix of salt and sweet. The popcorn only increased the intensity of my appetite, so I decided to call it a night and get a takeaway for the train home.

When I announced that I would have to leave, he got up to go to the toilet and said, "Can you pay for the tab, and I'll get you outside?" *What?* Me? Pay for the tab? The cheeky fucker. I had travelled two hours to see him and find out he had already eaten, then I was going to have to take a two-hour journey home, and he wanted me to pay for the full tab! The penny dropped. He hadn't forgotten about dinner, he just didn't want to put his hand in his pocket. The selfish arsehole.

I pretended I only had £20 on me, and he had the cheek to say he wasn't getting paid until the next day and could he owe me one. I couldn't believe this was happening. What a nerve he had! Turning up on a date, knowing he didn't have a penny but insinuating he did by setting up a tab. There was no way I was ever going to meet him again. I was too angry to say any more.

Now, I knew that the bar was his local, so I was very tempted to print out his face on a warning poster. *Beware ladies: he is a tight-arse. If you see this man, tell him he is a using bastard.*

I coughed up for the six drinks, the £25 train ticket, plus the takeaway for the train home. It turned out to be a pricey night for someone who was not worth a penny. Ungentlemanly, rude, and the biggest TIGHT-ARSE going!

Namaste the fuck away from me.

TB Chat

Jane – Well, I paid for the full date last night
Senga – I don't feel sorry for you, you need to stand up for yourself and stop spending money on men
Weejo – Typical Jane
Louise – Did he not offer at all?
Jane – He said "Get the tab." and went to the toilet. I should have done a runner. I'm learning, I promise!

Tips

1. If you live a distance away, meet halfway.
2. If you are asked to get the full bill, say you don't have enough money to cover it. You could also pay your half and leave the manager to deal with your date's situation.
3. Plan dates on payday or the beginning of the month. Third week into the month could lead to you sharing complimentary popcorn at a bar.

Glossary

** Raging: Mad, not happy*

On a limescale of 1-10, that's weird

If you think I've exhausted all types of dates then you would be wrong. Have you ever come across a partner with obsessive-compulsive disorder (OCD)? Well, I have had to put up with my fair share. Here are a couple of the OCD men I have had the pleasure of knowing.

I dated a man called Samuel who would not speak to me while eating dinner; he would only commence the conversation once the last bite was well and truly swallowed. *Lovely – all about what you want then.* As soon as my plate was empty, he would whip it out from my hands, wash it and put it in the dishwasher. I am a chatterbox, so it felt very odd to sit in complete silence while eating. It made me wonder about the monks who take a vow of silence. The spiritual practice is known to improve self-knowledge and lead to a more harmonious life.

Well, I can tell you the twenty minutes of silence just made me think of ways to make him crack up. What would he do if I started talking with my mouth full of food, or if I spilled some sauce on the carpet? Oh wait, that's a kind of self-knowledge.

How funny – it does work! I once opened my mouth to speak to him after I had finished my food, and he looked at me as if I'd just killed his dog. To be fair, I do know a lovely park where we could bury him next to Leon's cat, Jack (my mind was wandering as you can imagine).

Samuel had reservations about me staying over. I genuinely had to beg him to let me stay at his place one night, as I didn't want to drive the ninety-minute journey back home in the dark. After what felt like a court trial where I laid out the pros of staying over and the cons of going home, he eventually gave in and let me stay. Oh, how lucky I was. Don't worry, Samuel, your feeling hesitant about me staying over was a great confidence boost for me.

During the night, Samuel was agitated and refused to cuddle up – clearly someone had issues. As soon as his alarm went off in the morning, he stripped the bed and put the sheets in the washing machine. I had literally just opened my eyes and was forced out of bed; it made me feel very unwelcome. That was enough of an insight into his life for me. His OCD was too much. I don't want to have to worry if a biscuit crumb falls onto the bedsheets. On the plus side, at least my home would have been sparkling clean if I had lived with him. I wasn't scared of him. He wasn't intimidating or violent, but the condition had clearly taken over his life.

The NHS website states that obsessive-compulsive disorder (OCD) is a common mental health condition where a person has obsessive thoughts and compulsive behaviours. OCD can affect men, women, and children. Some people start having symptoms early, often around puberty, but it usually starts during early adulthood.

Another person I dated called Gary would inspect my shoes as soon as I entered his home. If my shoes were dirty, he had to clean them. At first, it was a novelty. I mean, I felt honoured to get my shoes scrubbed for free. He used to be in the military, where it had been drummed into him to have spotless shoes. I started to wear different shoes each time I saw him so I could get them cleaned – a win for me and a win for him since he enjoyed it so much. He would lay out a newspaper on the floor, take my shoes and carefully inspect them.

His other unusual OCD habit involved participation from me – he got me involved with cleaning his shower. Any time I went for a shower, I had to clean it before I exited. The apparatus of choice was a window scraper. I had to get rid of all the water from the top and make sure the glass was see-through by the time I came out. I was the guest, but I felt like his unpaid cleaner.

Now, we all know the first thing you want to do when you come out of a shower is to grab a towel and get warm... well, picture me, freezing and cleaning his shower in the buff. I'm short, so it was difficult to reach the top of the shower and scrape all the water to the bottom. I began to feel anxious in case I was doing it wrong.

Why didn't I just tell him to piss off? I always try to please the date I'm with and not be rude. There are certain instances where I should have point-blank refused. I was cleaning his bloody shower, I felt like Cinderella and not the part where she becomes a princess... what the hell? The first time I questioned him about it, he was very matter of fact and said it stopped limescale forming around the shower – a very old-person thing to say. I suggested he did one big clean in the shower every week, and he looked at me as if I was a madwoman.

I started to question if I was being a bit lazy when it comes to cleaning. Maybe once a week is seen as disgusting? Sometimes, I don't clean my shower for months. Surely, the water cleans it every time you shower? I didn't mention the cleaning process again. Maybe it was normal, and all people put up with the shiver to have a sparkly clean shower?

It wasn't until I told my friends and heard their uproarious reaction, that I realised I would be getting slagged for this for a while. My friends could not believe I had been cleaning his shower. One of my friends peed herself when I told her (she had just had a baby, so her pelvic muscles were weak).

At least now, when I do get round to cleaning my shower, I'm a bit of an expert.

Silver lining and all that.

Tips

1. If you have been asked to do something you find odd, say no. There's nothing wrong with saying no. If you accommodate that person's rituals, it can actually make their condition worse.
2. If you are in a relationship with someone who has OCD, help distract him or her from their thoughts. When they get the urge to do something compulsive, suggest going for a walk or watching a movie.
3. Do not blame them for having OCD. You can get mild forms, which can be easy to cope with. Blaming is not good for your relationship. Instead, celebrate any small steps they achieve.

The wife factor (lockdown special)

I have to be honest, lockdown dating hasn't been great for me. There is only so much you can ask before the conversations get monotonous or boring. Let's face it, we aren't doing anything exciting. If you're working from home, you basically go from bedroom to living room, to bathroom, to kitchen and repeat each day. The person you're speaking to hasn't been out of their house or if they have, they have been to the supermarket or on their daily walk. The conversation starts to get stale.

The dating app I use is called Hinge, it's created a new feature during lockdown where you can select a video call from home, it means you don't need to give out your number which is always a relief as some men can appear 'normal' online then you swap numbers and instantly regret doing that when they turn out to be creepy, needy, or vulgar.

I got chatting to a guy called Barry. He was good-looking and seemed to have decent chat during the few days we had been messaging. He asked if I would like to do a video call. *Wow, that's soon but I guess I'm not doing anything else.*

Interestingly, he mentioned he was an introvert which made me smell bullshit. A video call is not a trait of someone who is shy (first red flag). I felt like it would be daunting to speak to a stranger on a video call but I guess this might be the 'new normal'.

Anyways, what's the worst that could happen?

Well, let me tell you. Barry sent me an invite to Zoom. Weird right? Very formal (second red flag). I wonder why he didn't suggest speaking through the video app feature. The topic on the invite said 'Barry & Jane introduction'. Now, by the end of this story I had a few suggestions for a different topic heading.

On our chat feed, he said he would be wearing casual clothing (third red flag). I mean, of course, I would expect him to be in casual clothing, unless a suit or kilt was his usual attire for his dates. I replied saying I was gutted as I was hoping to put on my ball gown - no reply (fourth red flag, Barry didn't seem to have a sense of humour).

The time was approaching for our 'Zoom date', and I was starting to feel weirdly excited as I wanted to see what other odd things he would be coming out with. Also, it would provide new chat for my girls since none of us had any new gossip.

Barry's opening line was 'Thank you for joining the call, tell me a bit about yourself', (fifth red flag, I didn't know I had to whittle out my CV), it was like an actual interview. I then rattled off what my job entailed and he followed up with some questions. He seemed satisfied with what I had to say, *phew ... I can take a deep breath now*.

Barry explained I was his fifth Zoom date that week, wow he's a busy bee (sixth red flag, he seemed to be a serial dater). He then went on to proudly tell me he has a Tinder badge (seventh red flag, not something you should boast about pal).

He explained that Tinder awards you with a badge if you have a high number of swipes. He achieved one-hundred-and-twenty-two swipes in seven days, so his profile now displayed a badge to prove his popularity, now that's worth noting on your CV or cover letter. Not sure if he was talking bullshit but it definitely wasn't turning me on. He then went on to explain he had certain criteria he looks out for on the calls (eighth red flag, to even mention the word criteria to my face shows he's ruthless and a prick).

1. Can he picture the girl as someone he could marry
2. Is she someone he could introduce to his family
3. She can't live out-with Glasgow, maximum he will travel to see a girl is thirty minutes. Sorry for anyone who lives thirty-two minutes out, you may be the girl of his dreams but unfortunately, you've missed out - gutted for you!

He was upfront at telling me he rates each girl after the chat (ninth red flag, certain facts should be kept to yourself). The majority of girls he spoke to that week got a 6/10, I wonder what my rating would be, would I be a perfect ten?

Zoom calls are the future for his dating process. He doesn't want to waste time on meeting a girl in person if she doesn't match up to his expectations. When he decides to meet a girl in person he wants her to be sober for date one and two so he can analyse the girl, if a girl initiates a kiss on the first date then he loses respect (tenth red flag, it seems to be all about his needs). He's the polar opposite of a romantic date. So if there was any sexual chemistry, you basically have to hold off to date three. At least you know you didn't have to shave your vagina for date one or two.

After our call had ended, he messaged to ask if I was wanting kids and marriage. He really is interviewing for a potential wife. I replied saying that was an intense question, which he agreed with but mentioned it was important for him to know. You'll be pleased to know I passed the first round and he wanted to arrange a second Zoom call. I didn't have any interest in this guy with the amount of red flags that have been flared up. I am delighted I won at something that week of lockdown. I'm curious to see how many girls he keeps for the final round.

TB Chat

Jane – I've just made it through to the next round of a zoom date
Louise – I'm so glad I'm not single, was he nice?
Weejo – virtual dating is the new normal apparently
Senga – fuck that, is he fit?
Jane – he was odd, he interviewed me, the new normal is a terrifying thought

Tips

1. If you feel like your virtual date isn't going well then maybe do a Jackie weaver* and boot them out the call.

2. If you recognise too many red flags then probably best to move swiftly on.

3. If a date has certain demands then it looks like they probably won't compromise easily.

Glossary

** Jackie Weaver: Mrs Weaver became an internet sensation after clips of Handforth parish council were shown during a chaotic meeting on Zoom. She won the fans of millions of viewers when she would remove members from the call if they were out of line.*

Not enough? Here are lots more hilarious antics from my friends...

“ 1. I was seeing a guy for about a month, and while we were getting intimate one night, he accidentally coughed in my face and his grog* landed on me. As I was screaming, he sucked it back up. I genuinely don't know what was worse – that I had green slime on me or the fact that he sucked it up and swallowed it again. Men are boggin*.

“ 2. I had a date with a guy who picked me up in his Porsche, which I was impressed by. We had arranged to go to the cinema then have dinner. After the cinema, he asked if he could come back to mine, which I declined, as I don't sleep with a guy on the first date. He was pissed off and started speeding down the streets and told me he was dropping me home as he had better things to do now. I asked if he could stop somewhere so I could get a takeaway to take home with me.

He said he didn't want me to smell his car out, but he did agree that he would pull in at the nearest supermarket. To piss him off, I got chicken wings from the hot food counter. As I got back to the car, he told me I couldn't bring the food in and would have to eat my food outside the car. There I was eating chicken wings while he was sitting in his Porsche waiting for me to finish. Let's just say, I kept some chicken grease on my fingers and wiped it on his seat.

“ 3. I was having a lunch date and the guy said he didn't have enough money to pay for the meal. I said I was happy to go halves. He suggested I paid for lunch and he would get the drinks. When we went to the bar to order drinks, he brought out a money bag of coppers and counted them out. It was mortifying. Safe to say, I was never going on a date again with this penny pincher.

“ 4. I turned up to meet my date for the first time to discover he was wearing filthy trainers. (Note from Jane - I know someone who would love to clean those). They were scruffy, dirty, and had holes in them. During the date, he went outside to have a cigarette on four occasions, he left me sitting inside for ten minutes each time. Every time he returned, I got a stench of the smoke on his clothes.

Rude, unpresentable, and stinking.

Luckily, on dating apps you can now put if you're a smoker so it's definitely helped me whittle down the men more.

“ 5. I met up with a guy for drinks, and we were getting on amazingly well. He asked if I wanted to continue the date back at his and made it clear he had his own bar. When we got back to his flat, I discovered it was like a building site. It was being renovated and there was dust everywhere. To make it worse, I stood on a nail. My foot was gushing blood. I told him to show me his bar, so I could drink the pain away. His bar turned out to be a worktop with bottles of alcohol, not the bar I was expecting, what a disappointment.

He began to kiss me and we ended up having sex, no foreplay, which again was another disappointment. After he ejaculated, he literally rolled over and snored the whole night, what a selfish bastard. In the morning, he didn't even lift his head off his pillow to say goodbye. He just said, "Take care".

I messaged him later on that day and found out he had blocked me. Good riddance is all I have to say.

“ 6. Met a guy in a queue at a coffee shop. We both enjoyed each other's chat and decided to meet for dinner that evening. During dinner, he constantly talked about his ex and how she was an escort. I couldn't believe he was telling me this information. He mentioned that he still worries about her so copes by taking cocaine before work. If he didn't take drugs, he would feel anxiety about her wellbeing. I wonder if he was on coke as he was telling me way too much information, and come to think of it, he was very chatty.

To top it off, as we left the restaurant, he looked up at the building nearby and asked me if I had ever wondered what it would be like to jump off the top of it. On that note see you, pal.

"7. I went on a lunch date, and the guy ordered exactly what I ordered. *Kind of sweet*, I thought. When my burger arrived, I took the top of the bun off, as I get bloated when I eat too much bread. He continued to copy me, which I found odd. When I asked why he wasn't eating his bread, he told me he wanted to do exactly the same as me so we could get on better. As the Spice Girls song goes, *Goodbye, my friend!*

"8. I once got a six-hour train journey to spend the weekend with my close male friend and declare that I was attracted to him. We had hooked up once before and ever since then he had sent me flirtatious messages. I never flirted back as I didn't want to ruin our friendship.

One day, I had an epiphany and decided to tell him I wanted to be with him. In my head it felt like I was in a rom-com, about to declare my feelings and live happily ever after. Our weekend was great, we slept with each other, then I burst out crying and told him how I felt. His reaction was not what I expected; he didn't feel the same way and told me he was getting back with his ex. Hearing words like that makes you feel sick, making you want to instantly cry. I didn't want to appear upset as we had a whole day left to spend together. I muttered that I understood but I'd had to tell him just in case he felt the same.

It was the longest day on Earth. He was quiet, awkward, and didn't want to talk about it. That night, he slept in the spare room. I cried the whole night, feeling like such an idiot, wishing I hadn't said anything as I knew our friendship would now be over. Moral of the story, rom-coms are bullshit.

“ 9. I was speaking to a guy online, and he seemed fun and intelligent. I was so excited about our date, until the night before, he randomly sent me a dick picture. Now, our chat hadn't been sexual at any stage, so I was taken aback when he sent me it. The thing is his penis looked odd. The head was massive; it looked like a mushroom. I cancelled the date, as clearly all he was after was sex.

“ 10. I had been at an all-day festival and drunk-messaged a guy I had been sleeping with. He asked me to come by his place on my way home. As soon as I turned up, he started to take my clothes off. I told him I wanted to go for a shower as I had been dancing and sweating all day.

He said it turned him on knowing that I hadn't washed and asked if he could sniff my panties; he wanted to smell my sweat on them. He started to pull my panties off. I was gripping onto them, the thought of him smelling them was mortifying. His grip was stronger, so I had to watch him sniff them and put them in his mouth. It made me gag. He tried to kiss me with the pants in his mouth, wrong on so many levels. I had squatted next to the portacabin loos so you can imagine the state my knickers would have been in.

“ 11. A guy I had been messaging for weeks asked me if I wanted to go out on his motorbike for our first date. I was so looking forward to it as it was different and exciting.

The day before our date, we spoke on the phone, and he was telling me he had borrowed leathers off a friend for me, which was thoughtful. The next day arrived, and I hadn't heard from him. We were supposed to meet at 1 p.m. and it was 11 a.m. I called him and got no answer. I followed up with a text asking if he was okay.

Two hours later, he replied, saying he was hungover and not feeling well. I was raging. How rude to cancel because he was hungover! I replied instantly, calling him an arsehole which he wasn't happy about. He told me I was out of order and clearly didn't care about his wellbeing. He tried to pin it back on me by saying all I cared about was going on his bike, and I was selfish to try and force him to take me out while he was feeling dodgy.

He was instantly blocked, a waste of my time.

On yer* bike, dickhead!

“ 12. I was having sex with a guy, and he wanted me to put my finger up his arse. I inserted my finger, and all was going well. I was getting the noises I wanted to hear from him. As soon as I took my finger out, I noticed my acrylic nail had disappeared. For the next thirty minutes, we had to fish around in his arse trying to locate it. In the end, he had to resort to waiting for a poo to get the nail out.

“ 13. A guy wined and dined me in a lovely restaurant I had always wanted to go to. I knew he had money as he had an expensive car and a good job. After dinner, we went to get snacks to take back to our hotel room and that is when I caught him stuffing bags of sweets into his jacket pocket; I was shocked and mortified. When I got back to his car, I asked him why he had done that, and he said he got a thrill out of stealing.

“ 14. I met a guy online, and we agreed to meet outside the university library. In the distance, I could see someone waving inside the uni café. I went into the café, gave him a hug and sat down only to notice another girl there. I thought it was really weird that he'd brought a pal, but maybe she would leave soon. The conversation was odd. I was asking him lots of questions, but he wasn't asking me anything back.

After my coffee, I made my excuses to leave. As I looked at my phone, I saw a message from my real date who said he was outside the library. Unfortunately, it was too late and he had already left. I had sat down next to a stranger and probably his girlfriend. They must have thought I was crazy and just played along.

“ 15. I was set up on a date through a friend of mine; I was optimistic since my friend knew him. We decided to go to the cinema. As I was eating my popcorn (before the film started), he shushed me. The couple in front of us looked behind, thinking he was referring to them. He apologised and said he wasn't telling them to be quiet.

I was gobsmacked – it was the cinema, and everyone munches on food throughout the film. I quietly started to chew on more popcorn, and I kid you not, he grabbed the popcorn off me and put it down at his feet, saying the noise drove him up the wall. I excused myself to go to the toilet and didn't return.

“ 16. I used to have sex with a guy who wanted me to tell him stories about me shagging other guys, while we were having sex. It turned him on, but I got exhausted from all the talking. As soon as I finished the story, he would want me to tell another. I ended up having to make up the stories and tell him things I had never even done. He then called me a dirty slut and that was enough for me to storm out the room.

“ 17. My fuck buddy wanted me to pee my pants then let him sniff them. I didn't do it, but he would constantly send me messages asking if I could send him a video of me peeing myself. I'm sure there are websites for that.

“ 18. A guy I had been talking to for weeks said he would organise a romantic meal for our first date. He took me to McDonald's. I thought it was a joke and walked out the restaurant only to realise he wasn't behind me. I went back in and asked what was going on. He said he hadn't been paid yet but really wanted to meet me and take me for dinner. We were sandwiched between tables of kids who were spitting paper out of their straws. He wasn't worth the wait.

19. I was invited round to a guy's house who I had been dating; he said he was going to put his chef skills to the test. As I walked into his home, he asked if I could look after his kids (who were in the living room) until his ex came to pick them up. I was stunned – I had never met his kids.

I go into the living room to be faced with the kids staring at me. I asked them their names, and they did not mutter a sound. The five-year-old then started crying and shouting for Daddy. My date walked in and asked me why I had upset his wee boy. Lo and behold, that was the end of the date.

20. I had been seeing a guy for four months and brought up the subject of where the relationship was going. He declared he wasn't into labels and asked what was wrong with how our dating was going. I explained that I wanted to know where I stood and how I would introduce him to my pals. He then called me needy and said girls always need a label, '*you lot* are never happy' – Charming!

21. I kept bumping into a guy in the elevator in my building; we would casually smile at each other and travel the five floors in silence. Eventually, I decided to start a conversation, and from then on, we would chat anytime we saw each other. One day, he asked if I had a scanner. I didn't know if this was code for sex, so I got all glammed up for him to come round to my flat. Turned out, he did want to use the scanner. He was handsome but very shy, so I was trying all my best flirting techniques. On three more occasions, he asked to use my scanner.

This *had* to be a sign that he wanted to see me and was using this as an excuse. The last time he came round to mine, I launched in for a kiss, and we banged teeth. He never asked to use my equipment again. Obviously, he did only want to use the scanner.

“ 22. I arrived at a restaurant to meet a guy I had been chatting to online. I was very excited as he was gorgeous, funny, and blonde which was my type. I spotted him sitting at the table; I was so nervous. Then he spoke. His voice was high-pitched and nasal, sounding like he had inhaled helium. It was a complete turn-off. He's had the last laugh though as he is now married with kids, and I am still struggling to make adult choices.

“ 23. I was working as a dancer on a cruise ship and formed a relationship with one of the crew on board. One night, we were having sex, and his condom came off inside me. We didn't notice until it was too late. It took him a while to locate it and fish it out, his cum was all over his fingers. I wasn't on the pill, and we were out at sea for another day. We had to go to the doctor on board and get a prescription for the morning after pill – mortifying.

“ 24. I would regularly go to this nightclub in my hometown and would often see this gorgeous guy; we would flirt every time we bumped into each other. One night, he came back to mine, and we had incredible sex. The next morning, I asked what his plans were, and he said he was moving into his new home.

I asked how he felt about living on his own, and he said he wasn't going to be on his own – he was moving in with his fiancée. Wow, just wow!

“ 25. I was regularly shagging a guy who one night asked if I could lick his ass. I was happy to oblige. As I headed towards his ass, I smelt a strong whiff of shit. I did not know what to do as I had already said I would go for it … this boy clearly had not wiped his arse properly. I pretended to get a cramp in my leg and started to writhe around naked and in pain. I decided not to see him again to avoid being faced with an incident like that again. Please wipe your arse properly.

“ 26. I've had interesting experiences when it comes to being intimate, sometimes what you imagine is not what it seems when clothing is removed. I had been dating a guy called Kenny who was perfect, he was kind, affectionate, and a downright lovely guy. He had an adorable dog called Bertie that followed him wherever he went. I always think if a guy treats a dog well then it's a sign that they will be a decent person.

On our first date he said he wanted to get something off his chest as we were going to meet his friends who were drinking in a bar nearby and he knew one of them would tell me anyways. My nerves kicked in, *what is he about to disclose? Has he been in jail? Is he secretly married? Has he got a girl pregnant?* It was, in fact, that he had his penis tattooed. Okay well not too bad, but what did it say? Hopefully not suck it, my big shlong or don't bite.

Along the top of his shaft he had the word 'pleasure' written in italics. Apparently, he was drunk on a boys' trip in Ibiza and at the time, thought it would be a great idea. He mentioned it was always going to be a pleasure if he got a shag, so it seemed appropriate to choose that word along his ding dong.

He invited me to his home on date four, the night where things were going to get down and dirty. As we were getting intimate in his room, I peeled off his boxers. Whilst preparing myself to have the word pleasure coming towards my vision, out of nowhere his dog appeared on the bed, watching our every move. The dog was literally looking at me sucking on his dad's privates. I wanted to apologise to Bertie, I felt so awful.

I swear that dog tiptoed into the room, as I didn't hear a thing or maybe I was too focused on looking at his dick tattoo.

Kenny put Bertie out of the room, the dog then started to whine and then I felt bad. I couldn't concentrate as I was giving his dad a blowie. All I kept thinking was, *when will he stop whining?* Obviously Kenny had no issues with the whining, he was having the time of his life.

“ 27. I met up with a guy, purely for a hook-up. He had booked a hotel room and as we walked into the room, he asked me to get undressed whilst he went to the toilet. I was starting to take my clothes off when I could smell a whiff of shit, my date was taking a dump.

I rapidly put my clothes back on and quietly opened the door to make my escape. It was a huge turn-off and if he really needed to shit, he could have used the toilets at the reception area.

“ 28. A guy invited me to lunch after we had been speaking online for a week. He booked a well-known hot spot for food that I knew had good reviews so I was really looking forward to our date. As he welcomed me and we got over the initial awkwardness, he then proceeded to take a protein shake out his bag.

I asked if he always drinks before a meal and he replied that it was his meal replacement shake. *Excuse me?* His plan was to drink his shake as I ate, it was so weird. He said that he gained weight easily so he was on a detox. I was so baffled by all this, I couldn’t understand why he didn’t explain this beforehand and we could have gone for a walk or a coffee.

“ 29. It was time for my first date with a guy who was incredibly wealthy which meant I knew we would probably be going somewhere nice for dinner. We met at a posh eatery and the staff all knew him as he walked in. I actually felt excited that they were making so much extra effort with him.

The food and wine was ordered and I was engrossed in his conversation until his phone rang. He said it was a work call and had to take it.

Forty-five minutes later, he came back to the table.

By then I had already eaten my meal, his dinner was sitting there cold and I had drunk a full bottle of wine. I was trying my best to be understanding but I was so annoyed and I guess the alcohol didn't help. He sat down, asked the staff if they could reheat his food and said, "Sorry, work kind of takes over my life," and carried on as if this was a normality for him. I decided that men who still take work calls at any point throughout the night are not for me.

" 30. I had been casually seeing a guy for two months, when one night as we were getting intimate, he asked if he could lick my feet. I said I would rather he not as it wouldn't be a turn on for me but he begged and asked if I would let him try, even if it was only one time.

I said I would need to clean my feet and his reply was, 'No, the dirtier the better', which made me look at him in a different way. Not the loving way, but *is this guy for real?* He put my feet up to his face and started licking. I actually felt sick as I had been wearing trainers without socks, so I knew my feet wouldn't be smelling fresh. Watching him get so turned on and sucking my toes was enough to end my casual relationship with him.

" 31. I was backpacking in Australia and was at a beach party. I got chatting to a Canadian and we decided to go back to his hostel for a shag. As we approached his dorm, he realised he lost his key card. He said he had an idea and took me into the laundry room. We were kissing and ripping each other's clothes off, it was so passionate and exciting.

I began to give him a blow job and as he came, I threw up all over his dick. It was the nastiest tasting spunk I've ever experienced. It was like out of date milk, the tang was unbearable.

He then looked at me like I was the issue when, in fact, it was whatever he was eating that was unbearable. As they say, you are what you eat! Maybe he had too much asparagus.

" 32. I was looking after my sister's flat for a week. Whilst staying at hers, I arranged a date for that weekend. I really hit it off with the guy, so I invited him back to my sister's flat.

Her couch was too small so I resorted to having sex on her bed (not my proudest moment as I know I would be so angry if I found out she had sex on my bed). Anyways I was in the moment, the passionate wild sex commenced.

The guy clearly knew what he was doing as I have never squirted so much in my life, so much so that after sex I noticed the bed was soaking and also had a tinge of pee smell. He helped me flip the mattress and to this day, my sister still doesn't know and I hope it stays that way.

" 33. A man I was seeing used to slap and spit on my face. He was a lovely guy until we were in the bedroom. I told him not to slap me on the face and his reply was 'would you prefer if I dick-slapped you?' You try it mate and I'll bite it! As for the spit, I actually spat back in his face, which he didn't like. That showed him.

“ 34. I had managed to hook up with an absolute belter who I hoped to hook up with again. As we woke up in the morning, I was desperate to fart but was worried to move to the bathroom in case it slipped out.

I lay there next to him, clenching my butt cheeks. This in turn led to my lower body making this loud groaning noise, sounding like a noise made by a cow. I was horrified, a fart would have been less obvious (if silent, of course). He turned to me and said, “Sounds like you’re brewing a jobbie”. I wanted the ground to swallow me up.

“ 35. I was backpacking around Asia and one evening I went to a beach party and typically got very drunk. I saw this handsome chap but it turned out he couldn’t speak English. We communicated through charades which I interpreted as him saying I looked beautiful. It turned out he was asking for a shag, next thing we are heading to his hostel. No one was in the room as everyone was attending the party so we had a quickie on his bed.

He got his Instagram out to add me and it turns out he was from Peru, *awesome, I can tick that off my list of nationalities I have shagged.* We waved goodbye and I went back to find my friends who thought I had been at the bar. I still haven’t told them this story.

“ 36. I went on a date with a boy who was extremely nervous. He was bright red in the face and seemed anxious. As I arrived, he knocked over and smashed his pint of beer as he came over to give me a hug.

I pretended to him that I had done that before to try to ease his embarrassment, but he spent the rest of the date looking mortified, I noticed his hands were sweaty. He didn't have much conversation after the incident.

“ 37. I was travelling around Australia with my friend. One evening as we sat in a bar, a waiter brought over a bottle to the table, he pointed to two men who were smiling at us. My friend and I felt like we were in a movie, this never happens back home. We went over to thank the men, one was hot and one was not (always seems to be the case).

Both men were lovely and invited us back to a party. We all got in a taxi and as we approached the house, we could see a jet ski, motorbike, speedboat, cars - *who owns this place?* The hot guy said this was his place and he had a surprise for us. We walked in and heard, 'Hello', it was his parrot. Wow, pretty cool.

My friend was being chatted up by the not-so-hot guy and she was clearly raging. She pulled me aside and said, 'don't you dare leave me with him.' I obviously said I wouldn't but I did want time alone with the hottie.

He took me out on his porch, which had views of the ocean. I couldn't believe what I was seeing. He kissed me and it was very romantic.

My friend asked if we could leave, I wasn't ready to go, I was loving it. She got pissed off and took a taxi back to our hotel and the not-so-hot guy went home as well.

Oh and turns out there was no party, it was a line they used, sneaky but I wasn't bothered as I was having fun.

Hot guy took me upstairs and we started going for it, his cap fell off and he was completely bald. Oh, hot guy wasn't so hot.

As he rolled over to sleep, I wanted to leave, so I began to plan my departure. I carefully sneaked downstairs and I was doing so well until the parrot shouted 'Goodbye' very loudly.

Fuck off, you daft bird.

“ 38. I was having regular sex with my fuck buddy and to be honest, I wanted it to develop into something more. One night after he orgasmed, I asked him if he wanted to go out on dates (FYI, I heard the best time to chat to a man is after he cums, as he's relaxed and more likely to agree to things).

Unfortunately, the reply was not what I wanted to hear. He told me dating the same person wasn't for him as he liked to try new vaginas.

“ 39. I was lying in bed with a guy that I had been crushing on for ages. I couldn't believe my luck that I ended up sleeping with him, which was incredible. As we were cuddling up, a fart slipped out. I have never wanted the ground to swallow me up so much. I couldn't even disguise it as it was a loud and proud one. I literally froze and he said, "Oh, someone needs the toilet." I tried to laugh it off but inside I was dying of humiliation.

“40. It was my first time sleeping with a man who was circumcised. I had only experienced a penis with foreskin. I had no idea what to do with his little man when we were heavy petting.

I felt like it was dry and I started to worry I would give him a friction burn. I resorted to spitting on my hand and all this phlegm appeared. It was mortifying. He looked at me in disgust. His flagpole quickly deflated.

What else was I supposed to do? Put my fingers inside me to get some juice?

Glossary

** Grog: another word for phlegm*

** Boggin: Scottish word for disgusting, pronounced ‘baw-gin’*

** Yer: Scottish word for ‘your’*

Final countdown ... swipe right

As you can see, it's been quite a journey and eye-opening on many occasions. I always try and think of a positive outcome in a bad situation. Even though I've experienced unsuccessful dates, I unsurprisingly have positives from each and every situation I've been in with the men I've met. For example, the cat funeral, the positive is that it's nice to see that amount of compassion and the lengths owners will go to give their fur baby a cracking send-off.

The guy who asked me to rub his stubs, well good on him for being proud of those bad boys and having the confidence to let strangers give them a stroke, that courage will do him well in life. The date who had rubbed his baw sack on me at least provided me with a decent massage.

The guy who pissed on me, well the positive is I got it out the way at an early age, so now I know to refuse if I ever have the pleasure of being asked again to partake in watersports.

The man who broke a woman's vagina, obviously nothing positive about that situation, the plus is that I experienced my first morning date, which I actually would like to try again. It's more casual and you can use an excuse that you have work, a meeting etc. if you are not feeling the vibe.

My advice would be to learn your standards and stick to them. Dating is fun. If you have a bad date, laugh about it with your friends; it's something to look back on for a giggle. I am by no means a dating expert, what I do I have is experience.

You may find yourself in awkward situations, and sometimes you are let down by the person you're attracted to. Don't give up! Life is all about learning. You can find yourself in the same situations whether it's in your work life or with friends.

For me, I always rely on my gut instinct.

I would like to take this moment to say RIP Jack. I'm sorry I didn't attend your funeral but this is how I imagine your send off would have been. Enjoy your next life at the Rainbow bridge.

Good luck to my fellow singletons. You've got this!

I hope you get your happy ending in more ways than one. As it stands, I've just seen a guy who looks alright, good bio, and nothing suspicious ... swipe right.

Afterword

I would love to know what you thought of
30 Reasons To Swipe Left!

You can write a review with your thoughts at:
• Amazon
• Goodreads

Connect with the author:
Instagram: @swipeforeverafter
Email: janefultonauthor@gmail.com
Twitter: swipe4everafter

Printed in Great Britain
by Amazon

79947383R00142